FIET'S VASE

and Other Stories of Survival,

Europe 1939 – 1945

JEREMY P. TARCHER / PENGUIN

A member of Penguin Group (USA) Inc.

New York

✦

FIET'S VASE

and Other Stories of Survival,
Europe 1939 – 1945

ALISON LESLIE GOLD

Most Tarcher/Penguin books are available at special quantity discounts for bulk purchase for sales promotions, premiums, fundraising, and educational needs. Special books or book excerpts also can be created to fit specific needs. For details, write Penguin Group (USA) Inc. Special Markets, 375 Hudson Street, New York, NY 10014.

Jeremy P. Tarcher/Penguin
a member of
Penguin Group (USA) Inc.
375 Hudson Street
New York, NY 10014
www.penguin.com

Permissions and credits may be found at the back of the book.

Library of Congress Cataloging-in-Publication Data

Gold, Alison Leslie.
Fiet's vase and other stories of survival, Europe 1939–1945 / by Alison
Leslie Gold.
p.   cm.
ISBN 1-58542-259-2
1. Holocaust, Jewish (1939–1945).   2. Holocaust, Jewish (1939–1945)—
Biography.   3. Jews—Europe—Biography.   4. Holocaust, Jewish
(1939–1945)—Influence.   5. Memory.   I. Title.
D804.3.G64   2003   2003050754
940.53'18'0922—dc21

Printed in the United States of America
1   3   5   7   9   10   8   6   4   2

This book is printed on acid-free paper. ∞

Book design by Gretchen Achilles

CONTENTS

PART ONE

The Archaeology of Survival

1

PART TWO

What Slipped Through
the Fingers of Death

149

All the history that we saw on the map in the kitchen pours into us and we contain it, we display it like a map for others to look at and be history. . . . Go into the world, go build cities, go discover countries: go spread love, go give, go make magnificence, get and give light, save and join and piece together (as you did the bits of string and cloth and whittled wood to make your ship) . . . and put it combined and formed and shaped, into the world like a bottle with a ship in it. Gather the broken pieces, connect them: these are the only things we have to work with. For we have been given a broken world to live in— make like a map of a world where all things are linked together and murmur through each other like a line of whispering people, like a chain of whispers . . . a round, strong, clear song of total meaning, a language within language, responding each to each forever in the memory of each man.

THE HOUSE OF BREATH—William Goyen

PART ONE

The Archaeology

of Survival

After the Germans attacked the Netherlands at 3:55 in the morning on May 10 in the year 1940, the Dutch fought back. On May 14, in order to force the country to surrender, the German Luftwaffe bombed the historic Dutch city of Rotterdam, which was then the largest port of Western Europe. The word usually used to describe the effect that this bombing had on Rotterdam is "obliterated." One usually reads or hears this attack described like this: "The Luftwaffe obliterated Rotterdam." Which it had. Quite shortly afterward, when Adolf Hitler, the German leader, threatened to attack Utrecht next and other parts of the Netherlands in a like manner if the Dutch continued to fight back, the Dutch surrendered to the Germans and Queen Wilhelmina escaped to England. Quickly the German army occupied this flat, wet, atmospheric landscape that has contributed Rembrandt, Vermeer, van Gogh, Anne Frank and much more to the culture of the world.

As a consequence of the destruction in Rotterdam, a newly married young woman, whose husband had already come to Amsterdam, who eventually became a poet and translator and would one day more than forty years later become a friend—then a vital young woman of twenty-nine—came to Amsterdam to join her husband. Although not easy to find, they eventually found and rented rooms in the house of a Jewish doctor and his large extended family of sons, daughters and grandparents in the neighborhood known as the Transvaal area in East Amsterdam. She and her husband lived in these rooms for two years until they were able to find other lodging in an eighteenth-century house on the outskirts of Amsterdam, in which, it would turn out, she would live out her life, and happens to be still living there, well into the twenty-first century. Also renting a room in the doctor's house was a young Dutch girl whom my friend knew as Fiet. My friend would see Fiet coming and going on the stairway and they would cordially greet each other in passing. But the acquaintance went no further.

As the Germans tightened the noose around the entire country, they cast a separate chokehold around the collective neck of the Jewish people, many of whom were quite assimilated among the general Dutch population. One day the doctor and his family disappeared. My friend would later learn that they'd gone into hiding in a house on one of the canals. The fortunate doctor and his family would all survive, except for one of the children who never came back after the war. It was around the time that round-ups of Jews had begun in 1942 that my friend heard a timid knock at her door one dark, evil night, as Grüne Polizei and German soldiers and trucks had begun to fill the neighborhood, signaling that a roundup was about to commence. Because the entire neighborhood was on edge, my friend cautiously asked who might be knocking. A voice answered, "Sophie." My friend realized immediately that it must be the young girl Fiet, since Fiet was the nickname for Sophie. She opened her door and saw Fiet standing in the hallway clutching a small suitcase.

My friend invited her to come inside. My friend no longer remembers exactly how she felt or what emotion Fiet showed and takes great pain to not dramatize or overstate the corresponding emotions. It seemed that the Germans had begun knocking on all Jewish doors and giving people twenty minutes to pack a rucksack. She explained that hers had been packed for months in the event that they came to her door. The whispered word was that

Jews were being deported to the East. Fiet held out the small suitcase and asked, "Would you keep these things for safekeeping for me until I return?" The unsaid fact—that Fiet was asking my friend to commit a crime—had entered the uncomplicated equation of being merely neighbors, since the entire Dutch population had been informed in no uncertain words that a Christian helping or abetting a Jew or Jewish property was a crime and would be punished harshly. (The adverb "harshly" needn't have been included, since everything the occupying German military did, they did with harshness.) Fiet had added, "And if I don't return, please keep these things." My friend doesn't recall what—if anything— else was said, or if she simply reached out her hands, took the suitcase and hid it somewhere in her small room. My friend gave her word to keep the suitcase until the young girl returned to retrieve it. Her thoughts at that moment? She doesn't remember them anymore, or didn't by the time I met her. But, knowing her kind character, she probably asked the young girl if she needed anything to take with her. Food? Clothing? Could she do anything else to help? As there was a crime against the Nazis now between them, there was also a promise now between them, and Fiet was already hurrying away to her appointment with fate.

Years later, one of the several young children of my friend discovered that the suitcase contained a tin of tea, a folded kimono, a small silver vase engraved with scenes of bucolic life. But before the contents of the suitcase were known to anyone but Fiet, almost the entire Jewish population of their quarter of Amsterdam was deported to parts unknown. Three more years later, when the war was finally over, and the few surviving Jews and others who had been sent to parts unknown—now gruesomely known—returned, the young woman named Fiet, who would have been

Fiet's vase.

twenty-six by then, was not among them. As survivors straggled back in the months after the Liberation, my friend waited for a knock at her door, searched on her own, hoping to return the suitcase directly into Fiet's hands. Even after a year or more, as occasional survivors trickled back to Amsterdam, my friend still hoped. Years and then decades passed, but Fiet never was seen or heard from again and no one ever came to claim the belongings she'd left for safekeeping.

Sixty years later, the suitcase, kimono and tin of tea are long gone. My friend has no memory any longer of how they disappeared. A few years ago, as she approached her ninetieth year, because of my interest in this dark time of Dutch history now fading from collective memory, she gave the remaining silver vase to me for safekeeping and I promised that I would pass it to someone else—to transmit it from generation to generation—before I died. She told me the few things she knew about Fiet: She was a Dutch girl of twenty-three. A Jew. She was probably a student. Fiet was short for Sophie. I wrote this information down on a slip of yellow paper and put it inside the vase. The harrowing statistics of what was lost and how it was lost in this war are well known. This small silver vase as the sum total of what remains of one young woman at the prime of her life is one immutable remnant that has survived from one unrepeatable life whose traces have otherwise been erased.

Fiet's small vase stands on my east-facing bookcase. Its darkened silver presence is like a stone in my shoe. To keep my promise, this vase will accompany me to the end of my life, as will the heavy memory of the human survivors of World War II—Jewish or other—I've encountered. Not one survivor I've engaged understands why he or she survived and another didn't. In my interviews with the subjects, in their memoirs or biographies, in the documentaries or other memorabilia on which this book is based, they all describe walking through the eye of the needle of fate at its cruelest and somehow—as bodies of loved ones as well as strangers fell around them—coming out alive on the other side. Each vivifies some configuration of factors that they speculate might have intervened to spare them from almost certain death, factors like unusual resolve, family bonds, human kindness, uncanny luck, even instances that can be viewed as supernatural. Though grave damage had been done to every part of their beings including their souls, each survivor's indelible voice extols the strength of the human spirit and the victory of a life wrested from extinction.

Although there have been two hundred forty wars—large and small—since 1945 and ominous conflagrations rage at this moment, World War II continues to stick in history's throat. Neither do we seem to be able to swallow this epoch nor spit it out. It is known in such accuracy and picked over in such detail because—among mountains more—four hundred eight-five tons of filed German records buried deep in mines and hidden in castles in the Harz Mountains were unearthed to provide information. Moreover, a multitude of partially burned files were found at Berchtesgaden and elsewhere at the end of the war, including stenographers' notes of top-secret meetings and conferences. Vast libraries of documentation of this time including diaries, documents, testimonies, transcriptions of conversations, lists, accountings, interrogations and the like remain intact as well.

World War II officially began on August 31, 1939, when, using their own man dressed in a Polish military uniform, the Nazis faked an act of aggression on a German radio station. In reprisal, early the next morning, on September 1—with surprise and unprecedented speed—the German military attacked Poland by air and by land at once. Within twenty-four hours, one hundred thirty Poles had died, another one hundred eleven by September 2. On September 3, in the small village of Truskolasy, fifty-five Polish peasants were shot. In the village of Wieruszow, also in Poland—setting the stage for what has since become known as the Holocaust—twenty citizens were forced into the market square because they were Jewish. A young woman—Liebe Lewi—saw her father being herded with the group. She ran toward him. Seeing this "impudence," as the German officer referred to the daughter's emotional response, at gunpoint, he ordered Liebe to open her mouth. When she did as he'd ordered, he aimed his pistol at her tongue and fired.

On September 3, the British and French declared war on Germany. That night, ten airplanes flew from Britain across Western Europe into German airspace dropping thirteen tons— 6 million pieces—of paper from the air onto German soil. On these leaflets was written: *Your rulers have condemned you to the mas-*

sacres, miseries and privations of a war they cannot ever hope to win. The warning went unheeded. Quickly the war spread. A little less than six years later—in August 1945 as atomic weapons arrived on the world stage—came the final surrender that ended World War II.

By the shores of a bay there is a green oak-tree; there is a golden chain on that oak; and day and night a learned cat ceaselessly walks round on the chain; as it moves to the right, it strikes up a song, as it moves to the left, it tells a story.

There are marvels there: the wood-sprite roams, a mermaid sits in the branches; there are tracks of strange animals on mysterious paths; a hut on hen's legs stands there, without windows or doors; forest and vale are full of visions. . . . And I was there. I drank mead, I saw the green oak-tree by the sea and sat under it, while the learned cat told me its stories. I remember one—and this story I will now reveal to the world.

PROLOGUE TO *RUSLAN AND LUDMILA*

—*Alexander Pushkin (Dimitri Obolensky, translator)*

UNUSUAL RESOLVE

*And Samson took hold of the two middle pillars upon which the house stood,
and on which it was borne up, of the one with his right hand, and of the other
with his left.*

—JUDGES 16:29

Naxos is where a young Greek named Iakovos Kambanellis
was born and would spend his childhood. The story of the
Labyrinth is set on the island of Naxos in the Cyclades in Greece.
Using the rich culture of Greece, Kambanellis would eventually
gather fame as a writer of Greek plays and be invited into the
Greek Academy. When he and I met face-to-face in Athens for
drinks on a hot afternoon, he told me, "Almost no one knew, until
twenty years after World War II had ended and I finally was able
to speak and write about my experience, that I had spent three
years in the labyrinthine SS concentration camp Mauthausen in
western Austria, wearing a red triangle." A red triangle was the
sign that he was in Mauthausen as a political prisoner. Although
he kept apologizing for his "poor English," Iakovos was a com-
pelling storyteller. He spoke easily, used hand gestures often and
lit many cigarettes. He'd take one or two puffs on the cigarette but

would seem to change his mind and quickly squash it out. Over cup after cup of coffee, his stories flowed and time flew.

As spring of 1945 came to Mauthausen, the young Greek Orthodox prisoner came to believe that the war was coming to an end. "In the last week of April we saw piles of papers being burnt near the part of the camp where the workshops were. They were burning the archives. Lists—of those who's been shot, hanged, gassed, drowned in the blue Danube, eaten by dogs, tortured to death—were disappearing." Daily the prisoners watched as hundreds and hundreds of bombers with American markings swept across the sky. Nightly, the prisoners could see splashes of light against the same sky. Staving off death, the prisoners tried to hang on, looked for every sign that perhaps the war might end before they did. Iakovos remembers that one severely malnourished prisoner dreamed that the *Kommandant* of Mauthausen had metamorphosed into a fish and was swimming strenuously behind the camp's rock quarry in a small tributary that branched out into the great Danube.

April passed. One night in the beginning of May the SS all disappeared, and on May 5 a dirty, battered tank rammed its way through the great wooden gate of Mauthausen. On top of the tank stood American soldiers like charioteers, aghast at what was being revealed below them. "We howled, tore our clothes, shook ourselves as if we were demented. We pushed and trod on each other so as to get close to the tank. A lot of us fell on it and kissed the charred metal while others beat their heads against it and wept. I felt two hands grabbing my legs. I bent down to see. Two Spaniards had thrown a kapo facedown and were skinning him with knives. Near command headquarters, we halted. The women of Mauthausen were coming up the road, an endless line. . . . And just as we had grown silent watching them, they too grew silent. Their faces were hairy from malnutrition, their heads shorn. They wore trousers and sacks filled with rags to keep themselves warm."

As the first days of liberation wore on, Kambanellis wandered the grounds of Mauthausen and watched—awestruck—as the liberators brought food and medicine on jeeps and trucks; he watched the unloading. He watched as the search for the escaping SS began. Among those most interested in revenge was his friend Andonis, also a Greek, from Ambelokipi in Athens. Andonis had quickly acquired an automatic rifle and waved it at Kambanellis, boasting, "I'll bring you an SS to play with." Kambanellis fondly remembers those vivid first days of freedom: "The kitchens operated nonstop and we snacked all day. The camp had filled up with bread, spaghetti, potatoes, corned beef, biscuits, chocolates, toothpicks, toothbrushes, toothpaste, contraceptives, jam, soap, photographs of Broadway dancing girls." Suddenly—as if from nowhere—birds could be seen in the trees in the woods surrounding Mauthausen. And birdsong could be heard again. No one knew why or where the birds had gone during the war, but it was a fact that they'd disappeared and now suddenly they began to reappear.

One of the first duties of the survivors was to dig up the pits of dead prisoners. A makeshift cemetery was organized in what had been a sports field. The unburied corpses were carried to the cemetery and attempts at identification were made. As Mauthausen had many political prisoners, captured Russian soldiers, captured partisans as well as Jewish prisoners, attempts were made to identify the separate graves with the appropriate cross or Star of David. Kambanellis later admitted, "Every now and again, though, we made mistakes burying them and instead of putting a cross on the Christians and a star on the Jews, we put a star on the

Christians and a cross on the Jews. The fanatics on both sides objected. Others said, 'In any case the dead understand.'"

Kambanellis remains troubled over the fact that liberation had come too late for some of the prisoners, for after the gates of Mauthausen were opened, people continued to die. He wrote in his memoir *Mauthausen*: "We had paranoiac thoughts. Why do they die since we are free, since the war has ended? We would take the dead person quickly from the hospital so that the other sick people would not see him. We would go to the carpentry shop to find a coffin. The women dressed and laid out the dead for hours on end and gave them all sorts of things to take with them. Even a comb, a clean handkerchief, cigarettes. They gathered flowers from the surrounding fields so that they would have them all the years that they would no longer see them. The coffin was unpainted. The clean planks of the coffin were covered with letters and messages for the other world: '*My adored parents—We are fine, I always hear your words at the train station telling me: "Look after Annette." For the rest of my life I will do nothing else.' 'My sweet Lotte—Don't leave me here alone.' 'My son—I walk night and day in Mauthausen and ask the earth where it has hidden your ashes. The others are leaving. How can I leave with empty hands?' 'Mara, Elena, Moishe, my good children—I have only one job to finish. Afterwards I will close the doors and windows of the house which have been open so long and I'll come. . . . I kiss you, my sweet children, my beloved children, I kiss you. . . . I kiss you.'* Then we carried the dead to the old stadium and delivered them to the thousands and thousands of Mauthausen's dead who lay in the same place."

The American liberators asked that each nationality elect one member because, until every survivor could be repatriated or sent somewhere else, the survivors must rule themselves and field their own problems. Kambanellis was elected by the Greek survivors to represent them. Approximately two hundred Greek

Jewish women and perhaps a thousand men were alive. Some of these men were Jewish, some were Orthodox Christian like himself. His job was to catalogue the names of Greeks who were no longer alive, to field grievances and quarrels, document atrocities, begin arrangements for repatriation to Greece. Perhaps thirty thousand people in total were alive when Mauthausen was liberated on that May day.

The first group to leave Mauthausen concentration camp as a group were the Spanish. First, there was a memorial service for the approximately eleven thousand dead; nineteen hundred Castilians, Basques and Catalans remained. The entire camp gathered in the square where a grandstand, which was decorated with flags, had been set up and the sun shone down. Speeches were made, addresses exchanged: "Pedro Manuel Jimenes, Plaza Santa Anna, Sargasso," wrote Mr. Potocznik. Then Mr. Jimenes wrote: "Stefan Potocznik, Ulica Sienkiewicza 65, Krakow." A line of trucks—with signs on their sides reading TO MADRID or TO BILBAO or the like—gunned their engines. After the Spaniards had climbed into the trucks, they drove off one after the other. A feeling of sadness rather than elation was left behind. A few weeks later the surviving captured Russian soldiers gathered in the square along with the remaining population at Mauthausen. Again flags and grandstand, speeches and, this time, songs. The Russians had been great singers, were always singing softly with deep voices, sometimes barely murmuring but always singing. During their incarceration, the camp population had listened to these Russian voices with pleasure:

Winds and storms blow around us,
Children of darkness pursue us,

Now we're caught up in the next battle
And an unknown fate awaits us . . .

On the day of their departure they sang these words again, then marched out of the gates of Mauthausen along the roads that had been paved using the ashes of their comrades and other dead. For every living Russian soldier, at least thirty or forty had been starved or tortured or worked to death.

Kambanellis began the work of preparing for the Greek departure. He came to understand that only the non-Jewish Greeks wished to return home. Most of the Greek Jews did not wish to go back to Greece but wanted instead to go to Palestine—as the land that would become Israel was then called. This meant that they would have to wait in Mauthausen until illegal arrangements for such a journey could be made, because what was then known as Palestine was closed to almost all Jews wishing to enter. A few days before the Greek departure date, his friend Andonis walked into the room that Kambanellis was using as an office. He was carrying several bundles and bluntly told Kambanellis, "I'm leaving. Give my greetings to our homeland." "Where are you going, Andonis? Why don't you wait a little bit longer so we can all leave together?" asked Kambanellis. Andonis replied, "I'm thinking of changing direction." Seeing the puzzled look on Kambanellis' face, Andonis explained, "In Greece I used to sell fruit off a barrow. If I go back I'll do the same. It's hard for someone to change in his own country. But I can't go back to the same work. I think I'll burst. I've thought about it carefully. Seeing I've found myself in Europe, it's better for me to go to, say, France or England or America or Africa or Australia. The world's small and life's ridiculous. So up and at 'em!" Kambanellis remembers that they shook hands, embraced. A car was scrounged up into which five at the most could squeeze, but nine Greeks squeezed in or held on to the sides. They drove the car through the open gate of Mauthausen, taking Andonis to the village train station a few miles away from the camp. Then Andonis hoisted up his bundles and climbed onto the train. The friends sang:

> *That's life, Andonis*
> *That's life*
> *Companionship*
> *That sheds its leaves . . .*

and wept openly and waved. Then the men watched their admired Andonis wave back, framed in the window of the slowly moving train as it began its journey.

A few weeks later, on the day that the Greeks were to depart Mauthausen, the sun was burning. All the nationalities remaining in the camp had gathered to bid the Greeks farewell. The platform was festooned with flags, and the usual round of farewell speeches began as the sun beat down. The loudspeaker crackled as one of the speakers emotionally spoke: "In the five years that I stayed shut up in here, Greece sent freedom three times to knock on the door of Mauthausen. The first time was when we learned that Mussolini had been defeated in the mountains of Albania. The second was when the message reached here that the Greeks had climbed up to the Acropolis in Athens one night and pulled down the German flag. The third time was that day when here, right near us, in the pit of the stone quarry, a Greek named Andonis . . ." At the sound of the name "Andonis," cheers and shouts broke out and feet stamped for a man who the crowd would shortly discover had already gone back out into the world and was no longer among them.

Fifty-five years later as we sat across from each other at the Grand Bretagne Hotel in Athens, Iakovos Kambanellis lit one more cigarette and quickly stamped it out. His eyes grew glossy when he mentioned the name Andonis. He sadly shrugged in the Greek way when I asked if he knew what had become of him. "I lost track of Andonis after he departed from the camp. I heard later that he probably left for Australia but that's all." "And why was Andonis so beloved in the camp?" "I will tell you why." He began his story of Andonis in April of 1944, when a French prisoner came to the barracks filled with Greeks and told them there was a Greek in solitary confinement in the punishment hut. Curious to know if there really was one of their own inside, two gutsy Greek prisoners got as close to the punishment hut as they could and created a sham argument between themselves in Greek, saying things like, "If you're Greek say it. Long live Greece!" Shortly, as they were passing the punishment area, still arguing, a man came close to the barbed-wire separation, singing a familiar song in Greek:

And if you don't find me
take the boat and come,
my sweet Maritsa,
I'll be at Kastella

This was Andonis from Ambelokipi, who never stopped singing.

Once identification had been established, he would sing out information to the tune of a popular Greece song:

I was three days
In solitary, they
Brought us on Tuesday
From Dachau where
I'd been for ten to
Sixteen months
Zachariades was there
And that General of Metaxes'
Papagos—If there's cigarette butt—
If there's a butt
Throw it this way
But take care

Hearing this, Kambanellis remembers that he and his friends bartered two potatoes, cigarette butts and some bread with margarine from the black market. Then they wrapped the lot in rags like a big soccer ball and prepared they were passing the ball back and forth. When it seemed like the coast was clear, they passed it right over the barbed-wire fence into the punishment yard. The next day when they saw the man doing hard labor on his way to work at the stone quarry, the new Greek prisoner placed his hand over his heart as a gesture of thanks. Then off he walked to the dreaded quarry, where he and the others would be forced at gunpoint to descend at a run down the stone steps into the quarry. Then, with very large blocks of stone hoisted onto their backs, they would be ordered to run up the steep stairway to the top and even a quarter of a mile farther along the path. There were over two hundred steps in the dreaded stairway. These prisoners were made to do this work for twelve hours a day until they either dropped dead or were able to march back into the camp.

Stone quarry, Mauthausen, Austria.

One day the entire camp began to buzz with excitement. The name "Andonis" was on everyone's lips. Kambanellis remembers hearing about Andonis' astonishing encounter with death from several Serbs who lived in his hut. It seems, as he remembered the story, that on a particular workday—by noon—at least seventeen Russian POWs and Jews had already died performing the grotesque tasks of carrying blocks of stone up the two hundred steps at a run. If someone gave up, he was dragged away and shot. At one point in the early afternoon, a Jew carrying a large block of stone stumbled and almost fell. Seeing this, Andonis had given a signal to the man to come close to him. Then, Andonis held his own block of stone with one hand—and with the other, lifted up the Jew's stone. An SS witnessed this and ordered the Jew to hoist up another stone. The Jew did so. The SS shouted at him, "Run!" The Jew climbed up a few steps but because of the enormous weight of the stone block, fell to his knees on the stairway, letting his block tumble away. At that moment, the SS shot the Jew in the head and turned his attention on Andonis, who looked fearlessly at the SS. Andonis picked up the dead Jew's stone and added it to his own load and climbed the steps at a run. The eyewitnesses knew that this was the end of Andonis when the SS shouted at Andonis, "Come close!" with a lunatic look on his face. The SS went from stone to stone down in the quarry until he found one that was huge, probably twice as large as any other. The one he picked was a block so large that—all could see—it seemed like no mortal could possibly lift it.

As Andonis approached, the SS waved his revolver. The end was obviously about to come. But rather than approach the huge stone the SS had selected, Andonis stopped in front of an even larger stone block. "This is mine!" he announced, and to the disbelief of all, hoisted it up on his back. The SS stood agape as Andonis carried the great block up the stairway at a run, and—for the rest of the afternoon—carried the heaviest blocks he could find. Andonis' end did not come and he became a hero to all. Later, awed fellow prisoners would ask him, "How come, Andonis? How come he didn't kill you for making a fool of him?" To which Andonis would reply, "Aah, that bastard thought I'd sit down and let him walk over me. From that moment something went wrong with the SS. His engine broke down. They've all got a little engine in their heads that was put there in the SS school. They open their skulls and put this little engine inside that Hitler invented. It turns them inside out. But . . . if it breaks down . . ." And he would shrug. This was the only way he could explain why his life had been spared. And, of course, he had no way to explain how he had summoned stunning strength to lift humanly unliftable blocks of rock and carry them at a run up two hundred stone steps again and again and again.

When Kambanellis finished relating his long-ago memories of Andonis to me that afternoon, the cocktail drinkers had gone and the place was almost empty. The waiters were tidying up. He had to go home because his wife was expecting him and we walked through the marble lobby of the hotel together and out into the street that bordered on Syntagma Square. I found the street noise of car horns and motorbikes jarring and abrasive. After we'd said our goodbyes and he was about to hurry away, I reached out my hand and stopped him because suddenly a question had come to mind. I asked him if Andonis was a Jew. "No," he replied, "he was Greek Orthodox." "And do you remember his last name?" He sadly shook his head. "No, I did not know his last name."

After arriving in the United States in 1947, Leo Bretholz went to Baltimore, Maryland, to live and continues to live there. This is where we met. When Leo speaks, his words overflow with fresh emotion. He looks about twenty-five years younger than he is. For a man who'd survived such hardship in youth, I was struck by the vibrancy of his physical appearance. For many years he owned and ran a bookshop in Baltimore but he no longer did when he sat with his wife, Flo, across from me at the table laden with food and drink in the dining room of their home. Although he last saw his mother almost sixty years ago, he continued for many years to meet and remeet her in a recurring dream that got no less vivid with the passing of time. He stopped having this dream only when he began to chronicle the memories of his wartime experience. In the dream, the streets of Vienna are filled with patrolling Nazis. Leo wishes to find a way to reach his mother and goes to the apartment building where the family once lived. He sees that men are demolishing the building. As he watches, wall after wall implodes until only a single wall of the building remains standing. Finally, this wall collapses, revealing his mother, who has been living behind it—secretly—for all the many past years.

Leo was seventeen on the Tuesday evening in late October of 1938 when his mother walked with him to the tram stop and waited for the Number 5 streetcar. The stop was several streets from their apartment building in a heavily Jewish working-class neighborhood of Vienna, Austria. His mother was forty-three, had been a widow for nine years. Leo was carrying a suitcase and an old leather attaché case. The plan was that he'd go to the city of Trier in Germany and then cross the River Sauer into neutral Luxembourg, where an aunt and uncle lived. He would be safe there. His mother had chosen a Tuesday because—being superstitious—she believed that Tuesday was a day that boded good luck. She had persuaded him to leave Vienna because, since March of 1938 when Hitler and his *Anschluss* had been welcomed by ordinary Austrians with rapture and joy, Jewish people had been beset by violence. She and many others believed that Hitler was a temporary aberration. She assured him that before too long, he would be able to return home.

As it happened, Leo spoke not a word about his travails for fourteen years after the war had ended, and even when he was able to speak, he wasn't able to return to Vienna until 1970, after thirty-two years had elapsed. What he found in Vienna was exactly as he remembered it, as if there'd never been a war. It was the Vienna embedded irrevocably in his deepest memory. But it was devoid of each and every human being he'd ever loved. His escape was not as simple as he and his mother had envisioned that evening in 1938 when she watched him climb onto the Number 5 streetcar, never to see him again. Instead, for seven harrowing years, crisscrossing parts of Luxembourg, Belgium, Switzerland and much of France, Leo audaciously wriggled out of noose after noose as each was placed around his throat by the pursuing Nazis and their collaborators in Vichy, France. To this day he doesn't know where he found so much brazen courage. As for his constant resolve to survive through those years, it had been plentiful indeed.

His mother's last words to him were "Be very careful! Take good care! Write as soon as possible!" Dusk had turned to dark, and lights were being lit across Vienna during the short streetcar trip to his grandmother's apartment. Grandma's last word was his name, said through tears—"Leo!"—when he left for the train station to which his uncle Isadore and aunt Rosa took him through drizzling rain by taxi. Their final words before the train began to move into rain that had become heavier were *"Bleib gesund!"* Stay well! For the next twenty hours Leo sat in numb silence in the dark train compartment facing two equally silent Catholic nuns as rain scored the compartment window. It was afternoon when he disembarked in Trier, in the Moselle Valley, and though the rain had stopped, heavy gray clouds quickly gathered again, and soon more rain fell until his clothes and body were sodden.

Leo was assisted on both sides of the River Sauer by a paid smuggler driving a Peugeot. This had been arranged for by a committee called the Ezra that existed for the purpose of helping Jews get into Luxembourg. Wearing a blue gabardine raincoat, a suit, knickers, shoes and socks, Leo studied the River Sauer. Because of the constant rain, it was swollen, cold, widened; its brown water swirled with tree limbs rushing downstream. The smuggler told Leo to put a dry pair of socks into his pocket, and, without help from the guide, he struggled across what should have been a muddy trickle but had been turned into a swirling torrent. Quickly the depth dropped from under his feet, the water washed over his head. Pulled by the current, Leo was forced to swim for his life, his luggage and clothing acting like deadweights pulling him down the entire way. On the Luxembourg side, thoroughly drenched, he waited for the smuggler to pick him up in his car and drive him down a country road to meet Leo's aunt Mina at a pre-arranged place, a tavern outside the town of Echternach. The smuggler drove Leo—still soaked—and Aunt Mina to Luxembourg City, where she and Uncle Sam had lived for some time.

Leo believed he'd be safe in Luxembourg. He'd turned his back to Nazi Austria and Nazi Germany. Free France and Belgium were not very far away. It was 1938, Europe was still at peace. But on the second day in Luxembourg, the police arrested him in a café while he was having breakfast. After one night in a prison holding cell, two policemen took him to Mondorf-les-Bains. They watched while he crossed a footbridge into France. After careful thought, under cover of darkness Leo doubled back to his aunt and uncle in Luxembourg for a brief stay, then, driving for one entire night with a carload of fellow escapees, he was smuggled into Brussels. At one point in the journey he turned back eastward in the direction of Germany and Austria (now annexed to Germany) and saw, "in the farthest perceptible distance, odd coloration streaked against a dark horizon. It could not have been a rainbow because it was still dark. We saw flashes of color, as if the sky were being finger-painted by some invisible giant. One of the other passengers in the smuggler's car shouted, 'Look at the sky in the distance!'" It happened to be late at night on November 9, 1938, infamous Kristallnacht, when Hitler gave the order to burn synagogues and began the assault on Jewish people and Jewish property.

Belgium seemed an oasis. Leo went first to Brussels, then was moved to Antwerp, where he fell in love for the first time with a girl named Anny. He was able to remain in Antwerp at 68 Lamoriniere Straat, living in a room above a bistro until May of 1940. After war began on September 1, 1939, although tension mounted, Belgium was not yet involved. However, on May 10, 1940, in Berchem Hospital in Antwerp where Leo had been admitted the previous day to undergo hernia repair, he woke before the operation had begun to the sound of sirens and explosions and was told to leave his hospital bed and the hospital immediately. Bombers from the German Luftwaffe were overhead. All the patients who were ambulatory were told to go home. On the same day, Leo was arrested as a foreign national and taken by train to an internment camp in southern France at St. Cyprien on the Mediterranean Sea. In August 1940, he crawled through a hole made in the sandy soil under a barbed-wire fence at St. Cyprien. From there, he walked to the town of Perpignan where he took a train to the spa town Luchon in the Pyrenees Mountains near the Spanish border. It was here that he stayed until November, when all foreign nationals were ordered to leave Luchon for Bagnères-de-Bigorre, forty miles to the northwest, into which large numbers of refugees flowed.

In March 1941, Leo had his twentieth birthday in Bagnères. He moved to a small town named Cauterets even closer to the Spanish border, where he stayed until they began deporting Jews

Leo Bretholz in Antwerp, 1940.

to the infamous Drancy internment camp. Under cover of darkness he avoided arrest and deportations. A day later he sneaked back to hide with friends at Bagnères. He had to walk all the way, stopping in a field at Lourdes at dawn. In Bagnères he lived in hiding, reached his uncelebrated twenty-first birthday and there he acquired false papers. He became Paul Meunier, an eighteen-year-old French boy from Strasbourg. He began to hatch a plan to escape by foot to the safety of Switzerland with his friend Albert Hershkowitz, originally from Lodz, Poland—also the holder of false papers and a false identity.

Leo and Albert began their escape on October 4, 1942. Wanting to look like ordinary Frenchmen, they wore French berets. They took the train to Evian-les-Bains in the French Alps, where they contacted an underground guide who—for a price—agreed to guide them across the Alps to the Swiss border. The grueling journey went smoothly except that by the time they'd walked to four thousand feet, Leo's feet had become acutely painful with blisters. Reaching the summit of the trek at dusk, they were able to view the inviting lights of Switzerland below as well as the serenity of Lake Geneva. The sight of ordinary electric light was quite uplifting, as all of Europe was blacked out behind them. Paying off their guide, Leo and Albert easily crossed the French–Swiss border near the small village of St. Gingolph. Despite intense foot pain, Leo experienced great joy at the crossing. Albert was so happy that he began to sing. With new energy, spirits elated, they strolled toward their destination on Swiss soil.

After barely a half hour had passed, a Swiss border policeman appeared out of nowhere. He wore a green uniform and a stiff round hat, and held a large shepherd dog on a leash. "Your papers," he demanded. Taking one look at them, he uttered, "Come with me. You are here in Switzerland without authorization." He escorted the boys through St. Gingolph directly to the police station and interrogated them. Despite terrible pain at doing so, Leo removed his shoes. His feet were so swollen and had bled so badly that blood and skin and socks had become one. Abysmally desperate, Leo fell on his knees, begged and kissed the hand of the sergeant to please not deport him. It was to no avail. The gendarme continued to interrogate them, then—after about an hour—sent them back to the French side. There they were confined to a cell by French police and, the next day, were escorted by train to an internment camp that was barely twenty miles from St. Cyprien, from which he'd escaped a year and a half before.

The new camp was a dirty, squalid place named Rivesaltes. It was at Rivesaltes—sensing that doom awaited him—that Leo became obsessed with thoughts and plans for escape. On October 20, 1942, his determination became even stronger when he was again transferred. He was sent behind the barbed wire and guard towers of Drancy, near Paris. There, amid dysentery, vermin and human misery, an obsession with escape festered. In November, word raced through Drancy that his group was going to be "resettled," which, rumor had it, meant either hard work or something unknown, unnamable. The rumor was true because, along with a thousand others as a few brave prisoners sang the "La Marseillaise," Leo and his frail friend Manfred Silberwasser were taken by bus and truck to the small train station of Drancy–Le Bourget, through which I have many times benignly passed on a suburban train, luggage at my feet, on my way between Charles de Gaulle Airport and Paris. Leo's unrelenting thought was escape. He was part of Transport Number 42, destination Auschwitz, Poland. In 1978, as he noted in *Leap into Darkness,* Leo acquired a record of deportations from France—*Le Mémorial de la Déportation des Juifs de France*—which listed those on Convoy Number 42 who had died and those few who'd survived. The name "Leo Bretholz" was among the dead.

As evening approached, the crowd was counted out into groups of fifty. Each group was pushed at gunpoint into a railway car meant for freight. Leo boarded with his friend Manfred. The car contained one bucket only for waste that was quickly filled, saturating the entire car with stench. Though he'd been given some bread, a chunk of Gruyère cheese and a tin of sardines, there was no water at all. Leo was pressed by the crowded conditions into a corner of the car underneath the one small, barred window. Although he and Manfred were both from Vienna, they'd lived in different neighborhoods and hadn't known each other before Drancy. His friend Albert was also in the freight car. As the first night passed, gray drizzle fell outside the window. Leo's despair mounted when the train sped up. He could not take his eyes off the window, which was rectangular with bars, about sixteen by twenty-five inches. Albert sadly sang, *"Non ti scordar idi me, la vita mia legata è a te."* Don't forget me, my life is tied to you. Some people prayed, *"Oy, Ribono Shel Olom."* Master of the Universe. People muttered or wept or cursed or whispered to a child or loved one throughout the night. A young man, obviously in love, kissed tears from his beloved's face. This man had a bandaged leg that had begun to stink, had probably turned gangrenous.

Leo suggested to Manfred and Albert that they try to escape through the window. Albert declined, his spirit of defiance had dissipated. Manfred was willing. He and Leo debated the possibility while additional arguments pro and con flew at them from other captives huddled together: "You'll be killed." "They'll punish the rest of us." "It can't be done." "There's nowhere to hide out there." A woman with a crutch who was clutching a young child on her lap pointed her crutch at Leo, *"Allez-y, et que Dieu vous garde!"* Go ahead, and may God watch over you! "When?" asked Manfred. "Before we cross into Germany," Leo replied. He reached up and pulled on the bars with all his strength. They were iron, solidly embedded and immovable. Manfred also tried. They tried together until veins popped out on their arms and temples. Traction was needed, so Leo stripped off his sweater and threaded it through the bars, twisting the cloth to serve as a tourniquet. But nothing budged. He tried his belt—no tension, no traction. Moisture was needed for traction but none was available. There was no fluid in the entire freight car except for the fetid bucket already filled and overflowed with sloshing human waste.

Even in his seventies, and though his father had been dead since 1930, Leo can still remember his pale, sickly father, Max Bretholz, quite well. He remembers that he loved to play dominoes and smoked incessantly. He remembers the sewing machine he used in the tailoring business. But it wasn't the dominoes or the cigarettes that he remembered, it was his father who remains vivid to this day. One time, near the Danube, when Leo was six or seven, he'd witnessed his father striking a man across both shoulders with his cane after the man had shouted at Leo, "Jew kid."

Suppressing feelings of nausea and his gag reflex, Leo dipped his sweater into the pool of urine that had collected beside the overflowing bucket, soaking it, then wrung the sweater out. Manfred did the same with his sweater. They raised their wet sweaters over their heads, threaded them through the window bars in tight tourniquets, and—urine and pieces of sticky feces dripping down their arms, onto their faces and necks—they achieved the traction they needed and began twisting and pulling and trying to jar the bars from the frame as the train rumbled along the track toward the border. For five or six hours, through the daylight hours, Leo and Manfred worked at loosening the bars. Again and again they wetted, wrung out, twisted the sweaters through the bars, their arms, hands, shoulders aching with the effort. Just before dusk, Leo noticed that the revolting excretion that was dropping onto him was mixed with metallic bits of rust. This meant that the iron bars had begun to loosen from the frame. So he and Manfred worked even harder and loosened the bars further and further. Finally, the two iron bars bent away from their frames—one up, the other down.

After dark, Albert took Leo into his arms in an embrace, wished him luck. Then Albert and Manfred hoisted Leo up to the small space now open in the window and Leo squeezed—shim-mied—through, twisting his body. Climbing outside, he grabbed onto an iron ladder along the side of the train. Manfred handed Leo his rucksack and squirmed out also and hung on beside Leo. The dank night air rushed against their faces. Leo could see the bright spotlight trained by guards moving left to right against the side of the freight cars. He prayed that the train would slow down while rounding a bend in the track, before the spotlights caught their profiles, so that they could jump. If they jumped at the pres-ent speed, Leo estimated that they'd be crushed. The wind was against his face, he imagined that they must be at the very eastern edge of France, in Champagne by now, not very far from the bor-der with Germany. Finally, as he hoped, the train slowed as it met a curve in the tracks and Leo saw Manfred leap from view. Aware that his heart was hammering frantically, Leo let go and jumped.

Reexamining that long-ago night, Leo recalls telling Manfred quite soon after they'd jumped, "Thirty years from now, when we think about this, it will seem like a dream." He remembers that Manfred had replied with sarcasm, "How can you think of thirty years from now when we don't even know what tomorrow will be?" to which Leo says he earnestly enjoined, "Because nothing is impossible any longer. After that train, nothing." Which was true because from that day on, through the remainder of the war, Leo operated with brashness that he had previously not imagined in himself. In his own words: "I was now a miraculous athlete, a pro-fessional escape artist, a young man in perpetual flight. I was indomitable. Also, I was too terrified not to run for my life." He further explains, "I felt miraculously freer than I'd even been in my life but wondered—Free to do what? Free to go where?" As soon as he'd leaped from the train, tumbling onto the ground, Leo heard the sounds of gunfire, heard whistles, heard the grinding of gears and saw that the train was slowing and coming to a stop several hundred yards farther along the track. He lay low in the dirt, heard footsteps and voices of soldiers searching, cursing in German. He held his breath until the voices died down and then heard the creaking clatter of the wheels moving slowly again, then move quickly along the track. He watched the rear lights of the train curl around the bend and disappear.

Leo and Manfred spent the night near Mussy with the village priest, who sent them on to another priest in another village the next day. They slowly wended their way to Paris, which they reached on November 8, 1942. They obtained forged ID cards with fictitious names. Manfred's name became Roger Savary and Leo became Marcel Dumont. Continuing their journey toward the "free zone" via Tours, they crossed the Loire River by rowboat on a misty morning. The police near Joué stopped but released them, and they boarded a south-going train. Just after Limoges at Brive-la-Gaillarde, on November 27, Manfred decided to go his own way. He and Leo bid each other farewell.

Leo continued on to Bagnères-de-Bigorre, and there walked right into the arms of the police while exiting the station. Brazenly—in a moment when the policeman was inattentive—Leo dashed away. Finding a place to hide, he was forced to squash a rat with his own hands. He was arrested yet again in December and was taken to Tarbes, where he was surrounded by various criminals and shared a cell with a Swiss man who was serving time for manslaughter. On January 8, 1943, in handcuffs, he escaped once more, leaping out a bathroom window. When he hit the ground, he ran until he was so exhausted and fraught that he vomited and fainted outside a shop in the pouring rain. When he came to, he discovered that the shopkeeper was a friend of a friend who removed the handcuffs with a hacksaw and sheltered him. He decided—rain or not—to try to walk to Toulouse, and walked through the wet night.

Exhausted, hungry, disoriented, Leo was picked up by two gendarmes and taken back to jail. There he was beaten with an iron poker because the police wanted the names of those who had helped him during his escape. He never revealed them. While beating him, the police sarcastically remarked, "Fast legs, huh?" and hit him in the legs. This was to let him know that he was suffering the consequences for running away. The season passed. Leo remained in prison. One day he woke covered with sores and boils. In September, he was transferred to a hard labor camp near Septfond. There he broke rocks all day long, until in mid-October he and fourteen other prisoners were put on a train at riflepoint. The tenacious compulsion to escape remained. Although it was broad daylight, he climbed out a window of that train, ran between parked trains, hid, ran, feeling his heart pound. He was in the city of Toulouse again, knew the Toulouse railroad station because he had already been there on two previous occasions. He found a hiding place on the outskirts of the city. Again he appropriated a false identity. His fictitious birthday became October 25, 1925, making him younger than he was; his place of birth, St. Jouin-sur-Mer, Seine Inférieure; his new name, Max Henri Lefèvre.

Leo remained undetected for the remainder of the war in France at 13 rue de Rochechouart, Limoges, in a widow's spare at-

tic room. He wore his beret cocked across his forehead. He did
work for the Resistance and had one final harrowing moment in
May 1944 when his untreated hernia became strangulated and he
fell ill with excruciating pain in a public place. Against his will, an
ambulance was called and he was taken in critical condition for
surgery to the Centre Hospitalier Régional de Limoges. In his
groggy, agonized state he realized that as soon as they undressed
him, they would see that he was circumcised and know he was
Jewish. Of course he'd be deported. He was now entirely helpless,
he realized, as the anesthetic was being administered. When he
returned to consciousness after the surgery, a Catholic nun wearing a white habit—a nursing nun—was attending him. In terror,
he looked into her dark eyes. Had his secret been discovered? The

The false identity papers of Leo Bretholz—alias Max Henri Lefèvre.

nun spoke softly in a reassuring voice, "I'm Sister Jeanne d'Arc," she said. "As long as I am in this ward, you have nothing to fear." And Sister Jeanne d'Arc kept her word. He remained safe until France was liberated.

In March 1943, Leo had learned that one of his uncles—suffering from a delirium of persecution—had had a psychotic breakdown and was in a psychiatric hospital called St. Luc, in Pau. Though at the time he had been on the run heading south under his false name Henri Lefèvre, Leo made a stop in Pau. He'd last seen his uncle six years before in Vienna. He remembered a refined, well-dressed man, a linguist who wore a Homburg hat. At the psychiatric ward, Leo gave his uncle's name and explained that he was a friend, Monsieur Lefèvre. A nurse escorted him to an empty room and shortly brought a disheveled, bearded man into the room. The man was his uncle and did not speak a word and didn't seem to have any awareness of who or where he was nor any interest in his visitor. Leo sat with him nonetheless and was about to leave when suddenly his uncle spoke in French to the nurse, "This is my nephew." Fearful for his own safety, Leo looked at the nurse, wondered if she'd have him arrested now. But when she winked at him, he guessed that the nurse saw the tormented older man as confused and assumed that any words he spoke were confused too.

When the nurse left the room, Leo tried to tell his uncle whatever scraps of news he still had about the family. Suddenly his uncle shouted, "Family. Erna. Your mother, whom I loved. Martha, the humanist. My own daughter. Don't tell me about family." Leo asked, "What do you mean?" His uncle's face was engorged with blood. He was angry. "They are all against me. They blame me for the war. The war is long over and they won't tell me." "Uncle, the war is still going on." Then Leo tried to tell him that no one was against him, that one day the war would end and the family would all be together again. But the older man was incoherent and began to cry. "My uncle put his face in the palms of his hands, and the weeping became sobs that shook his body. Some piece of him knew that his daughter was behind barbed wire and also knew they were all trying to keep their sanity and even when the end of the war arrived there would be no grand family reunion."

He became visibly upset when discussing his uncle as we sat together in his dining room in Baltimore. "I touched my uncle's shoulder and tried to calm him. The nurse appeared and told me my time was up. The two of us, my uncle and me, as Henri Lefèvre, were each of us missing our identities in our own way. We were both muddling through an endless war. We hugged a wordless goodbye." Weeks later his uncle was deported and—along with almost all of the family except Leo—was never seen or heard of again.

Today the trip to the railway tracks leading into what was once the walled fortress of camps and subcamps known as Auschwitz–Birkenau takes under an hour on good highways or good trains from Krakow, Poland. Inside the gates busloads and carloads of visitors in groups and alone roam freely along vast rows of barracks, through displays of old suitcases, of human hair, record books and documents, past ruins of former crematoriums, gas chambers, past plaques, memorials, crumbling structures being restored. The well-tended grass on the grounds is thick and soft; its smell is pleasantly sweet. Once, none was allowed to grow lest hungry inmates grab handfuls and stuff them into their mouths. I've been told that classes of young, mostly German, students come here as volunteers to mow these lawns in summer. Where once German fathers and grandfathers wouldn't speak to their children and grandchildren about the shadowy past, now access to information about this time is easy to come by, and these volunteers work somberly. Walking the vast acres is wearying, and wresting the ghosts of the past from the landscape is daunting for those who experienced it and almost impossible for those of us who didn't.

A hundred miles away and almost sixty years ago—on April 25, 1944—two young men crouched among trees at the edge of a clearing waiting for a German patrol to pass. They had come from the fortress Auschwitz–Birkenau, had walked and hidden since April 7, and had finally arrived at Poland's border. Not fifty yards away was a lush forest that was the border of the Slovakian part of Czechoslovakia where many of us have traveled by train or car. The goal of these men at the time was to reach the city of Zilina. They were bringing information and a dire warning with them; a warning that they hoped would spare the lives of a million innocent Hungarians who would shortly die if their warning wasn't heeded.

The names of these men were Alfred Wetzler and Rudolf Vrba. They'd been running through a dangerous gauntlet for eighteen days dressed to look like Dutch businessmen, but by the time they reached that small stand of trees they were dirty and disheveled and unshaven. They looked as if they'd been sleeping in woods, barns, parks, as if they'd been in a big hurry. They were. If they'd known then that their warning would be received with cold indifference, their hearts would have broken. Instead, they were able to cross the border and reach Zilina safely, present the startling information they'd culled about Auschwitz, their naïve faith in humankind intact. In Zilina they were feted, clothed, washed, given hot breakfast in bed. It wasn't until weeks later when a sobbing, aged woman brought Vrba his breakfast on a tray and told him—"They're deporting the Hungarians. Thousands of them. They're passing through Zilina in cattle trucks!"—that his heart broke.

Today Rudolf Vrba lives in Vancouver, British Columbia. A professor emeritus in the Department of Pharmacology at the University of British Columbia, he has published articles in scientific journals. His is the author (with Alan Bestic) of an often reprinted extraordinary memoir, originally titled *I Cannot Forgive,* and has given damning evidence as a witness during trials of accused Nazis. He was born in the small town of Topolcany in Czechoslovakia in 1924. Very early in his life his family moved to another town that was called Trnava. When World War II began, Trnava was part of what was known as the Protectorate of Slovakia, which was sympathetic to Hitler. In March 1942—at age eighteen—he decided to try to escape and join the Allies in England or even join Tito in Yugoslavia. He was captured at the border and, because he was a Jew, was put in jail. Word of his capture must have gotten around because, lying in his cell, he heard a woman's voice at the barred window, "Mr. Jew . . . are you asleep?" He replied, "No." Then cigarettes and food were pushed through the barred window of his cell.

Vrba was sent to the Novaky resettlement camp, in Slovakia, from which he escaped. He was recaptured and sent back to Novaky. He was beaten for escaping. Next he was taken by train to the border of Slovakia. Here the Slovak Hlinka guards remained. Submachine-gun-toting SS took charge of the prisoners, pushing him along with eighty other people and all their luggage into a cattle car. At Zilina, a very old lady was added to their car. Near Czestochowa in Poland, they ran out of water. After that, only by offering gold and money—even wedding rings—would the guards give them drinking water. At Lublin, the doors opened. Outside stood dozens of SS wielding whips, canes, submachine guns. Men between the ages of sixteen and forty-five were told to get out. Amid shouted orders and slashing whips, husbands and wives, fathers and daughters, were separated. Rudi and a herd of men were marched through Lublin's back streets, and quickly the wooden gates of the concentration camp named Maidanek closed behind them all.

He was given wooden shoes to wear and worked as a laborer at Maidanek. Twelve days later, he was again marched through Lublin to the train station and—there—was pushed into a cattle car again with about eighty others. This time the weather was very hot and quickly the cattle car became unbearable. After the first day and night, all food and water ran out. Conditions and morale worsened for another two and a half days. Finally the train stopped, the doors were pushed open and all who were still alive were ordered out and ordered to line up and march. Vrba wrote about that moment: "I could see shrubs and trees. . . . Mentally I chalked up a point in favor of Auschwitz." He couldn't have been more mistaken, and very quickly realized it.

The SS in green uniforms lined the road through which the people marched. Shepherd dogs strained at their leashes; submachine guns and rifles were held upright. The scene was illuminated by a bright, steady searchlight coming from a watchtower. The people were directed to walk through the gates past a multitude of red brick barracks that had humorous carvings outside.

Aerial view of Auschwitz.

The streets had names—Cherry Street and Camp Street. He was taken to barrack Number 16, where he found two friends from Trnava already residing. They were Otto, who had once been burly and big, and Ariel, once a trim, elegant athlete who played the balalaika. Both were now gaunt, diminished, with sickly skin tones. They explained that they'd arrived months before in a transport from Trnava. Otto began Rudi's Auschwitz education right then when he explained, "We came in a batch of six hundred from Trnava. There are only ten of us left."

Vrba was tattooed with the number 44070, given a baggy shirt and trousers with zebra stripes and another pair of wooden shoes. Around him he saw the reality of Auschwitz—the "Moslems," as they were known, who shuffled like zombies. He observed the piles of dead getting higher and higher each day. He was lucky to be given a job in the food store. One day he saw his seventeen-year-old cousin, Eva, from Topolcany in a line of emaciated women being marched somewhere. He described the scene: "I called her name. Her head turned and she gazed, puzzled, unbelieving at me—'Rudi!' A whip rose and fell but Eva did not falter. I raised my hand and she raised hers in a gesture of splendid defiance; and, as she passed only ten yards away from me, she shouted once more, 'Goodbye, Rudi, goodbye.'"

After working at the food store, Vrba became part of a 1,600-man construction crew that worked so hard and were treated so brutally that after five weeks only he and a few other men were still living. He probably would have also succumbed had he not wrangled a job in the commercial area where the possessions of the incoming deportees were sorted and classified, the section nicknamed "Canada." "Canada" meant paradise because there was access to food, valuables, clothing. In this area, things were divided into piles—piles of pots, pans, shorn hair, eyeglasses. There were buckets filled with toothpaste squeezed in search of diamonds, buckets of currency, jewelry, gold. In various storerooms and yards with barbed-wire peripheries were mountainous piles of suitcases, rucksacks. Rudi saw a massive pile of probably 100,000 blankets, saw hundreds of baby carriages. His job was to carry piles of clothes wrapped in blankets from the unpacking stores to the section where they were sorted by young girls. He was beaten, had typhus, but didn't die. Day after day he watched thousands upon thousands of people herded into trucks that took them to their deaths, and he began keeping mental notes of what he witnessed.

When he saw ten thousand naked women marched away to be killed, he made a note. When the new concrete crematorium was completed, he noted the brick chimney with the yellow flame licking toward the sky. When he was assigned to a work detail in Birkenau—the adjacent camp—he noted the wooden barracks, the smell and sight of masses of disintegrating gray-brown slime-covered bodies in pits. He observed and noted the murder in September 1943 of four thousand Czech families who movingly sang the Czechoslovak national anthem, "Where Is My Home?" as well as the Jewish anthem "Hope" as they were taken to their deaths. At this point, Vrba's title was assistant registrar at "Canada." Because of his position he had much freedom of movement. On his feet he now wore good riding boots. He was nineteen years old at this point, physically fit, and fell in love for the first time in his life with a beautiful Czech woman named Alice who was shortly sent off to be killed.

Because of what he was witnessing, Vrba lived in a state of despair. Information had trickled down that a million Hungarian Jews, who had so far avoided deportation, were soon to be brought to Auschwitz and gassed. He dreamed of an escape that would bring this news to the ears of the world. Although he saw escape after escape fail, the men brought back either dead or—if alive—tortured, beaten, then publicly hung by way of lessons, a mad escape plan began to percolate in his mind. Rudi decided that he needed a partner and focused on a young man named Fred Wetzler he knew from his hometown. The plan was simple: On the ramp, accidentally, he'd discovered some loose planks under a woodpile and, underneath the planks, he observed that there was an area in which one could hide and move about unobserved. They stole the clothes—overcoats, heavy boots, well-cut, expensive suits that would look like Dutch businessmen might wear, a look he hoped would be inconspicuous out in the world. He discovered a method that would keep the dogs from being able to catch their scent. He found strong Russian tobacco. When marinated in gasoline and left to dry, the tobacco took on a strong odor that would throw off the dogs. He and Fred gathered provisions, since the plan was to wait in the hiding place for three days—or until the search was called off—and then to make their escape. Vrba assembled everything needed including a knife. He decided that if captured, he wouldn't allow himself to be taken alive.

Because he and Fred would need help moving the heavy planks, they bribed two Poles who they hoped would not betray them. And at the allotted moment though several days later than they'd planned—on April 7 at 6 p.m.—risking all, the plan went into effect. Vrba describes in his memoir: "For a moment we both hesitated, for we knew that once we were covered up, there was no going back." They quickly got into the hole, adjusted the wood planks and began spreading the dog repellent everywhere around them. "Free—or dead. I felt the keen blade of my knife and swore to myself that if they found me, they would never get me out of the cavity alive."

When the siren—signaling the discovery of the escape—sounded. Vrba knew that the siren would go on for three days, during which time the entire camp, inch by inch, would be searched again and again. Too tense to eat or drink, Rudi and Fred listened to boots pounding, dogs panting, to the scratching sound of nails against wood right above where they crouched. They listened as the search party moved away and then returned again. While the search continued, life went on at Auschwitz. They could hear the familiar sound of a transport of deportees arriving, the revving engines of fifty or sixty trucks filled with human cargo, then the sound of the trucks driving their cargo to the next stop, referred to as "showers" but—Rudi and Fred well knew—really gas chambers, to be followed by the ovens, where dead flesh and bone would be incinerated into ash and flare high into the sky.

One entire day passed like this. Then another. Still, neither of them could eat. At various times during the second day the search party was again above them. They could hear voices speaking in German. Then, unbelieving, they listened as the searchers clambered onto the woodpile and began to unpile the individual planks of wood. Listening anxiously, they realized that these Germans were only a few planks away from discovering their hiding place. They braced for capture, until suddenly the Germans abandoned their search and scurried off the woodpile.

Silence returned. The long hours of waiting for the search to be called off continued. At eight in the evening during the second night of hiding, just as they relaxed slightly, they had another unexpected surprise. In the distance they heard the rumble of airplane engines coming closer. Then the sound of exploding bombs filled the air. Could the Allies have come to bomb Auschwitz at last? Not knowing what was happening, or if now—after all they'd gone through—they'd be killed by an exploding bomb, they braced and listened to the cacophony, not sure whether to be elated or depressed, until they heard the airplane engines move off into the distance, and the noise of explosion receded until the silence of the Polish night returned.

After the war, Vrba lived in Prague. He studied chemistry and biochemistry. He doesn't remember the subject of Auschwitz ever being mentioned in those postwar years. He worked in Israel from 1958 to 1960. In 1960, while visiting London, he met an Irishman named Alan Bestic who lived and worked as a journalist in London. Bestic drew him out on the subject of Auschwitz, his imprisonment for twenty-one months and seven days, his escape, the thwarted report he and Fred had brought with them to freedom. Vrba's memory for detail was extraordinary. In this way, and with Bestic's initial help, Vrba began to write about those years past.

While waiting out the three days under the planks at Auschwitz, Vrba wondered whether or not, if they should succeed in their escape, they could even find their way to the border, since he'd arrived in Auschwitz by closed cattle car. His only source of orientation was one map he'd found and studied while working in "Canada." During the disposal of the possessions found in baggage of a particular transport, he'd noticed a child's atlas among children's schoolbooks and papers. Obviously the family thought that the child would be able to continue his studies wherever they were being sent for resettlement. He'd torn out a map of Silesia showing the old geography of the corners of Poland, Germany and Czechoslovakia. He'd studied the map and tried to memorize the path of the Sola River as it flowed north to south between Slovakia—Sol, Rajcza, Milowka—and Auschwitz in Poland and decided that he'd follow the meanderings of the Sola River in order to find his way back to Slovakia, which he estimated was about eighty miles away. So, while waiting under the ramp for the search to be called off, he hoped, if they could make the escape, that the information that he'd gleaned from a murdered child's atlas would be enough.

Finally, on April 10 at six-thirty in the evening, they heard a voice shouting from the watchtower, *"Postenkette abzeihen!"* Cordon down! He wrote: "The shout seemed to echo as it was taken up from tower to tower." The search for the two escapees had been called off. They waited until nine o'clock that night; then, after an interval of pushing and heaving, the planks moved sideways. "We could see stars above us in the black, winter, moonless sky."

After carefully returning the planks to their place, they took one last look at the silhouettes of Auschwitz—the watchtowers, high walls, the bright spotlight moving, always moving—and began to crawl on all fours in the direction of the forest of birch trees. They crawled across an eight-yard-wide sandpit that encircled the entire camp. Every nerve was taut as they crept because they knew that explosive mines had been planted at intervals in this earth and that it would be by chance alone if they weren't blown sky-high. They reached a wide bracken-covered moor. It was beginning to get light. They saw a sign: ATTENTION! THIS IS AUSCHWITZ CONCENTRATION CAMP. ANYONE FOUND ON THESE MOORS WILL BE SHOT WITHOUT WARNING! They crawled through a field of young corn. They saw a column of women prisoners with their SS escorts marching to work in the distance. Finally, after two more hours of crawling on all fours, they reached the forest and were able to stand upright in the safety of fir and birch trees.

But before they could really relax, they saw a large group of boys dressed in Hitler Youth uniforms trooping through the forest. The boys stopped marching and scattered around the forest, sitting on tree trunks and fallen branches, unstrapping their ruck-sacks and removing sandwiches, which they began to eat. Even though a light shower of rain began, the boys stayed where they were and ate their lunches until the heavens opened and a soaking rain poured down, sending the Hitler Youth elsewhere in search of shelter. Fred and Rudi trudged on through the downpour. They saw another group of emaciated, half-dead women prisoners be-ing marched somewhere through the wet woods by SS guards. Fi-nally, exhaustion overtook them and they lay down in a clump of thick bushes and slept despite the rain. They woke to birdsong and shafts of afternoon sunlight pouring through the trees into the woods and began walking again even though a very dark night descended on the forest.

In the middle of that night, they found themselves walking briskly on open land. The silhouette of the watchtowers of an-other concentration camp became visible in moving searchlights. They didn't know where they were. Because they traveled by night, they were often lost. They had given up on the Sola River and were trying to reach the Beskid Mountains that stretched along the border. They'd been warned to avoid the small city of Bielsko—it was crawling with Germans. But on the fifth night of their trek they found themselves in the center of that very city. They had trouble finding their way out of its confusing center. Fi-nally they threaded their way through the disorganized city streets but, as dawn broke, realized that they were instead trapped in the center of a small village called Pisarovice, and knew they were in trouble, knew that—for the first time since their escape—they needed human help.

Since the punishment for helping runaway Jews was death, Fred and Rudi were frightened but nevertheless crept among chickens and geese into the backyard of a small house where a Polish peasant woman peered out at them from her kitchen door. Filled with fear, she let them into her kitchen. When she apologized for her poor Russian, Rudi realized that she assumed they were escaped Russian prisoners of war. She explained that one son was in a concentration camp and another was dead. She served potatoes, asked for help chopping wood—which they gave— then dished out more mounds of potatoes and told them to sleep. In the middle of the night she woke them and served hot ersatz coffee. She tried to press a few coins into their hands. When they refused, she entreated them to take the coins—"Just for luck!" She pointed out the direction of the mountains and they began walking again.

Snow remained on the shady mountainsides. Vrba and Wetzler kept walking, hardly eating, drinking from streams. Days passed—eight since escaping Auschwitz, then nine. On the tenth day they saw below them the town of Porebka, which they'd also been warned to avoid. They stopped to rest against a tree because Rudi's feet were hurting and had begun to swell. Before they could catch their breath they heard the sound of rifles and realized that shots were aimed at them. On the next hillside, they saw German soldiers on patrol, dogs pulling at taut leashes. As bullets whizzed, Rudi and Fred ran for their lives. They ran uphill through thick patches of winter snow hoping to reach the summit of the hill. They dove behind large boulders as bullets smashed into the rock face. While the dogs growled and the soldiers chased them, they ran, sliding down a hillside toward a valley where a torrential stream roared with the runoff of winter snows.

Trying to get to the other side of the stream, they plunged into the freezing water. The shocking cold was awful. Finding

strength somewhere, they dragged themselves to the other side
and kept forging through three feet of snow and—even when they
reached the woods filled with dense, tall fir trees—kept running
beyond the time when all reserves of strength and endurance had
given out. "The thought of a last-ditch capture was unbearable."
Finally they could run no farther, collapsed and covered themselves with branches and bracken. The woods were silent again.
Soaked, exhausted, trembling with cold, they didn't even realize
that they'd barely eaten.

Vrba estimated that they must be close to the border. Although his feet were swollen, he and Fred trudged on through
woods and fields. The next day—head on—they encountered a
Polish peasant tending goats in a field. They knew she might be
afraid: She could be killed for assisting them, and she might fear
that they would kill her. Throwing caution to the wind, Vrba told
her the truth, that they'd escaped from a concentration camp and
were trying to reach the border of Slovakia. She told them to go
no farther, to wait in the field, that she would send food to them
immediately. Then, she added, when it was dark, she would send
someone to help them find the border. They watched as she
turned her back, walked down a hilly slope where she crossed a
bridge that was at least a thousand yards farther on. Could they
trust her? They admitted that they didn't, couldn't, but at the
same time realized they had no more strength to run farther because they were weak with hunger.

They hoped that if she betrayed them, at least they'd see who
was crossing the bridge and perhaps be able to run into the woods.
They stayed put. A few hours later they saw a young boy approaching on the bridge below carrying a package. When he
reached them he uncovered a pot filled with cooked potatoes with

pieces of meat and watched, amused, as they bolted down the food like starving animals. Taking away the empty pot, the boy promised that his grandma would soon come and walked back down the slope and across the bridge. Rudi and Fred stayed where they were. The temperature began to drop as night approached. After another few hours had passed they saw the old woman approaching from a distance. She was not alone. A man was at her side who, when they'd climbed up the slope and reached them, Vrba saw was pointing a gun at them. Grandma handed them another pot filled with potatoes, which, as they were still ravenous, they gobbled down quickly, keeping their eyes on the gun as they ate. Shortly the man began to laugh and shoved his gun into his pocket. He explained that by watching them eat like animals he could tell that they were really escapees from concentration camps and not disguised Gestapo sent in search of peasants who offered assistance to the enemy.

The man and woman took them home to sleep. At this point Rudi's feet were so swollen that he could barely walk. At their cottage Rudi used the sharp blade that was deep in his pocket—the knife that he planned to use to commit suicide if he was captured—to slice off the thick leather boots that encased his swollen feet. He felt immediate relief. The peasant reminded him that there was still much walking to do, then explained the schedules of the German patrols at the border. Germans were sticklers for schedules and never varied. If they took the Germans' routine into consideration, they'd know exactly when to cross over. He outlined this routine, then noticed Rudi's shoeless feet. He handed Rudi his worn slippers. A while later, Rudi and Fred and the peasant left in the dark and walked for another two days. The peasant was right about the German patrols, and each time they encountered an area that was heavily patrolled he took out his heavy pocket watch, knowing when the patrol would pass by so they could avoid it. Finally, he pointed to a forest fifty yards away— Slovakia. He suggested that they wait until the next patrol had passed before they made their dash. He wished them good luck and was immediately gone from sight.

So—courage and mission undiminished, wearing carpet slippers—Rudolf Vrba and Alfred Wexler hid in thick bushes and waited for the next German patrol. Their eyes never left the trees that stood fifty yards away. It was the morning of April 25. A Friday.

FAMILY BONDS

I am the family face;
Flesh perishes, I live on,
Projecting trait and trace
Through time to times anon,
And leaping from place to place
Over oblivion.

"HEREDITY"—*Thomas Hardy*

Beautiful, in her late teens, Jewish, with sparkling eyes, Rena Kornreich had caught the eye of many young men. She'd grown up on a farm outside the small Polish town of Tylicz. Her parents, Sara and Chaim, had two children—Zosia and Gertrude—right after they were married. Sixteen years after Gertrude, Rena was born, and two years later, when they were considered quite old, Danka was born. From birth Danka was frail and sickly. Very soon after her birth, Danka came down with croup. As the rest of the family looked on, the coughing stopped and Sara thought she had died. She covered the little one's face with a sheet. Suddenly, crying was heard from under the sheet. Sara pulled it back and saw that her Danka was alive.

After the Nazi occupation, anticipating trouble, knowing she and her husband were old and tired, Sara had said to her strong elder daughter Rena about her fragile baby sister, "I need you to look after your sister, Danka." Always obedient and devoted to her mother, Rena had given her word. But very quickly her promise was broken when, one day, German soldiers separated her from her family and deported her with a group of young women to the town of Humenne across the border in Slovakia. In Slovakia, her group was herded together with a large number of old and young Jews and other "enemies" of Germany and assembled on a train platform. Rumor spread that they were being sent by train to work camps. Despite the fact that she had no family or friends here, knew no one in this town, she always remembered how her eyes had longingly searched the faces in the crowd that assembled beside the platform for a familiar face. Her fervent hope was that somehow her family had found her. She examined every face, but all were strangers. As she was climbing not into a normal passenger car but into a freight car meant for cattle, oranges rained down, tossed by someone in the crowd. Rena reached out her hands and caught a few oranges. Then the door of the freight car was pushed shut and she was crushed against at least eighty people.

A man died in the night. Rena had never before seen death. The people pressed in the opposite direction in order to distance themselves from the corpse. But distancing was futile. The dead man's wife held his body against her and spoke with him as she would if he were alive, whispering through the entire night. Rena shared her oranges and bread with a woman who was nursing a child. The woman wasn't a Jew. She was a Communist, also hated by Hitler. As the first night wore on, the need for water became intense. By the second night, thirst was the consuming obsession of all and death was becoming commonplace. That was early spring of 1942. This first journey was the prologue to more than three years of incarceration that followed.

Half a century later, Rena and her husband, John, retired to the gently rolling foothills of the Blue Ridge Mountains of North Carolina; they reminded her of the Carpathian Mountains in Poland. In interviews in old age she was able to describe the sound of that first cattle car rattling against track and the horrific experience inside during the days and nights of that journey. "It is as if I'm in a tunnel with no light at the end and nothing to stop the onslaught of darkness. The faces around me have changed over the days until no one is far from losing control of their minds. It is as if the world has been shorn of color, the only hues in the spectrum being black, gray and the white of my boots. In this dank and fetid car I determine what I must do to survive. Everything that reminds me of what once was—my childhood, my past, my life— must be locked away in the recesses of the unconscious, where it can remain safe and unmolested."

Although thoughts of her lost family dogged her, as time passed her spirit flagged, and nothing began to matter anymore. Rena has no doubt she would have died had something not happened, to which she attributes her survival. By that time she had smelled the pungent odor of Auschwitz, had survived her first selection, been relieved of her possessions and been disinfected. Her beautiful hair had been shorn. She'd been tattooed with the number 1716, slept with bedbugs and lice, seen babies die, had— body and spirit—begun to starve. What mattered arrived at Auschwitz on a transport of 798 women from Brno, Slovakia, in which relatives of my own paternal grandmother might also have

Danka *(left)* and Rena *(right)*, with their friend Dina and a bear, before the war.

been. That day, Rena noticed the new arrivals, already separated from the men, tattooed, disinfected and shorn of hair, wearing green woolen shirts. As with all new arrivals, she studied the faces in line in the wild hope that there'd be a familiar face among them. She believes that it was her heart that recognized the figure in this line of women long before her eyes did, that what happened next gave her the will to stay alive. "At that instant of recognition I found my reason and will to live."

As the line approached, Danka—whose beautiful red hair had been shorn—hadn't recognized her big sister until Rena threw caution to the wind and gripped her by both bony shoulders. Rena squeezed, said, "Danka!" Hearing her own name caused Danka's knees to buckle. Although a hiding place on a farm had been arranged for Danka after Rena's deportation, when rumors spread that Rena had been sent to a work camp, she had willingly volunteered for deportation when the next call-up came with the purpose of joining her sister. Her transport had gone directly to Auschwitz and, despite the vastness of Auschwitz, and the change in her appearance, Rena had recognized her. "You're all I have," Danka told her sister.

It was quickly obvious to Rena that the frail, frightened girl who was only two years younger but seemed even younger wouldn't last long at Auschwitz. She remembered the promise she'd made to their mother. She believed that their fates were entwined. She talked the *blockowa*—the block elder—in charge into allowing Danka to live in her barrack. The first night in Block 10 in their shared bed, Danka lay engulfed in her sister's arms. Danka, already weakened by diarrhea and exhaustion, was bewildered, disoriented. Rena tightened her grip and spoke emphatically into Danka's ear in Yiddish: "Listen good to what I'm going to tell you. We're farmer's daughters. We're going to work, but that is what we do already. The work here will be nothing to us. And this is my dream, Danka—I'm going to bring you home.

We're going to walk through our farmhouse door, and Mama and Papa will be there waiting for us. Mama will hug and kiss us, and I'm going to say, 'Mama, I got you the baby back.'"

Three years and forty-one days later, on May 2, 1945, when American and Russian soldiers liberated Rena and Danka from Neustadt Glewe—a camp north of Ravensbrück where they'd been sent after Auschwitz and Birkenau—they were close to death. Their liberators took them to Ludwigslust, in Germany, then to a nearby refugee camp. From there, the girls were sent to a hospital in the Netherlands, where Rena and Danka would learn that they were the only two surviving members of their entire family except for one member who'd emigrated to the United States before the war. Since they'd grown into women in the meantime, it was here that they met and fell in love with two Dutchmen. Rena believes that her iron determination to keep the promise she'd made to her mother somehow tipped the scale between death and life for them both. She swears that this promise is what saw them through the general debilitation and starvation they experienced and helped them survive several particularly dangerous brushes with death.

The first of these events happened in Birkenau, where they were moved in late summer 1942. Birkenau, which was actually a division of Auschwitz, was only a mile and a half away. Rena couldn't remember if they were put into Block 20 or 22, only that Birkenau was harsher than Auschwitz. She had begun to have moments of detachment from her body and mind. She had begun to lose track of seasons and years at some point in the winter of 1943. Morale was so low among the prisoners, most of whom were covered with sores, abrasions, their clothes in rags, that nightly more and more of them would dash themselves against the electric fence, where their charred corpses would be left stuck to the live wires. One morning, as spring approached and it seemed that perhaps morale would lift, Danka woke with a chill and a scabby brown crust on her lips. Neither symptom mirrored either typhus or scabies, which were the most dangerous diseases in the camp just then. Though she tried to hide it, Rena developed chills and muscle spasms too. She learned that a new disease—being discussed in whispers only—had come to camp. It was deadly. Its name was malaria.

Just then, although illegal and dangerous to do so, Rena made personal contact at the work site—a bog where prisoners were digging and sifting sand—with two young Poles from Krakow. They passed a note to her. It said: *I'm Heniek. My friend is Bolek.* Intensely worried about Danka, dangerous as it was to communicate with male prisoners, she wrote back that her sister was terribly sick and she was desperate for help. Although she would never discover how these two young Poles did it, they somehow provided clandestine bottles of tomato juice, lemons and finally quinine tablets for Danka with another note: *Quinine three times a day. In a few days more juice. Be well. Love, Heniek and Bolek. (Bolek's in love with Danka. I'm in love with you.)* Remedies were hidden under a pipe for her three times more. As soon as the vitamin-rich lemon touched Danka's diseased lips, the brown crust dissolved. And, taken with the other gifts that contained vitamins and healing minerals, both girls quickly improved. Afterward, to thank them, Rena looked for Heniek and Bolek at the male work site, but they were no longer there. They had probably been transferred and were never again seen or heard from. She believes they appeared in time to save Danka's life.

Another dangerous incident revolves around a discarded pa-

per wrapper. It's hard to imagine that the red and blue paper
wrapper from a package of chicory might make the difference between living and dying, but Rena swears it did. In Tylicz, Mrs.
Kornreich added chicory, a plant with blue flowers and leaves
used for salad, to their coffee to make the taste smoother on the
stomach and remove some of the acid. Chicory's red roots, when
ground and mixed in with coffee, stained everything they touched
unless one quickly washed off any residue. One evening in Birkenau, Rena was scrounging in the garbage near the kitchen for potato skins or scraps to bring back to the barrack to her hungry
sister when she found a discarded chicory wrapper in the dirt.
Bringing it to her nose, she smelled the odor of chicory. It evoked
Mama, home, the nurturing moment of a cup of coffee. Hiding
the wrapper in the hem of her dress, she noticed that her fingers
were stained with the remembered red color.

It happened that, at the time, the women's camp was in a state
of high tension because word had spread that a very large selection was coming that would eliminate the many sick, depleted,
weak and starved, who would be gassed. It was less important to *be*
strong and healthy than it was to *look* as if you were healthy and
still able-bodied enough to work when you passed by the selecting
SS and were told to go either left—to death—or right. Rena was
very worried about Danka surviving the impending selection.
Danka had recently been hit in the face by the lid of the barrack
kettle when the guard had flung it against the wall during a tirade
and had been left with a gaping wound that bisected her forehead.
Danka's flesh was pallid and deathly white; she was also nauseated
all the time and weaker than usual from loss of blood. Logic told
Rena that Danka would never pass the selection, since women
who didn't even look as wretched as Danka were being singled

out for death. Remembering the chicory wrapper, obsessed with keeping her sister alive, Rena hatched a plan and used the residue of red powder to rouge Danka's cheeks and to cover the angry scar on her forehead. Immediately Danka's face took on the illusion of vitality and life. When the selection began, the sisters approached the Nazi doctor who wore an immaculate uniform and would decide which prisoner would go left and which would go right. Everyone in line had her eyes on his stony face as he stood still and waited for the line of woman to pass him. That day, neither sister was singled out as she walked past his piercing scrutiny.

Rena believes that the dream of returning Danka home to her mother had probably kept them both alive. After the war, when the sisters learned that there was no one alive any longer in Tylicz and no home to return to, they both married their Dutch boyfriends. After a few years in the Netherlands, the two couples immigrated to the United States, had children, grandchildren, lived productive lives. In America, seeing the number 1716 tattooed below her elbow, people—especially children—often asked Rena: "Is that your telephone number?" Eventually, she arranged to have the numbers removed by a surgeon. A small scar is left. Even in old age, Rena vividly, sensuously pines for and remembers her mother: "Her skin was so soft. I can still smell her as if she were standing right next to me. A blend of challah and vanilla extract, that is how Mama smelled." No clue to their fate was ever unearthed, though Rena assumes that, like most of their small Polish village, they were rounded up, sent to Auschwitz and—being over fifty at the time—most likely gassed. Their spirits continue to visit Rena. As she puts it, "Mama's and Papa's black shapes etched against the snow are engraved in my mind as if they are still there waiting for us to return, as if they always will be there, waiting. Tears usually taste salty but mine are bitter, frozen to the sides of my cheeks, frozen in time."

Although Romain Gary was not to learn the details until many years after the end of the war, his birth father (with his then wife and two children) died in a German concentration camp. The father, it was reported to him by an eyewitness after the war, had dropped dead of sheer fright while being herded into the gas chamber; his family presumably had been gassed. This was the man who'd abandoned Romain's mother in Russia shortly after he was born, whose name—during Romain's childhood in Moscow, in Vilna, in Warsaw and finally in Nice—was scarcely ever mentioned. The family name given him by this father was Kacew. His mother's Russian stage name had been Nina Borisovskaia. Later Gary would sometimes write under pseudonyms, François Mermonts for instance. But while living in Nice, mother and son invented the name "Gary," which they agreed was French enough, literary enough, noble enough and fittingly romantic all at the same time.

Madame Kacew concealed as many unpleasant or difficult aspects of her life from her son as she could. It wasn't until one afternoon when her face turned gray and she started to shake all over and then collapsed that he discovered she'd been hiding an advanced case of diabetes and the need for daily insulin shots from him for quite some time. Romain was terrified by the gravity of her illness. As he later wrote, "I felt I must hurry, that I had to write at top speed an immortal masterpiece which, by making me the youngest Tolstoy of all time, would enable me to lay at my mother's feet my laurels as a champion of the world, the reward for all her pains and labors, and thus give meaning not only to her life of love and sacrifice but to life generally, showing some hidden logic and cleanliness in it."

Being the sole means of support for them, his mother's life of sacrifice had included sewing costumes for dolls that were purchased by tourists in Provence, giving facials, clipping dogs, selling hats door to door, reading palms, selling jewelry in shops, running small hotels and pensions, and more, so that she could serve her son a rare steak for lunch every day, buy him a violin, arrange dancing and fencing lessons for him, and provide any and every luxury that she imagined would enhance his upbringing and future. At age twenty-four, Romain enlisted in the French air force. It was 1938. Although he was held back at first from receiving his pilot's commission because he was not French-born, he became a gunnery instructor at the air force academy in Salon-de-Provence. On the day war was declared, his mother stepped out of an old Renault taxi at the canteen where he was dining with his friends and—embarrassing him thoroughly—locked him in a theatrical, emotional embrace. She had brought him jam, sausage, ham, other gifts. She had not cared that the driver had taken five hours to get there and would take five hours to return to Nice, where she ran a small hotel-pension. With tears streaming from her vivid green eyes, she wished him "A hundred victories in the sky!"

She had come also to give him her blessing. Although she was born Jewish, she was Russian first and made the sign of the cross across his forehead with her hand, saying, *"Blagoslavliayou tiebia!"* I give you my blessing! It wouldn't be the first time that, after she had departed, someone would tell him, "There will never be another woman to love you the way she does." Romain was the first to admit that he was a mama's boy and had what he considered an abnormal dependence on this devoted, sacrificing Russian woman whose spirit accompanied him, as she'd done throughout his life, into combat. As he sailed with the Free French toward Africa to fight in Libya and Abyssinia, he would stand on deck late at night leaning against the railing, peering into the wake's churning, moonlit phosphorescence. He later claimed he viscerally felt the presence of his mother beside him at the railing smoking her ever present Gauloises. "I saw her by my side with such clarity that, more than once, I was on the point of reminding her that a blackout was in force and that it was forbidden to smoke on deck because of enemy submarines. And then, I smiled faintly at my naïveté, because I should have known that, so long as she was there beside me, submarines or no submarines, nothing could happen to us."

After training, Gary began his active military life as a bombing and navigation instructor in Bordeaux. Then actual bombing missions were ordered. He was wounded in the leg when refueling his Block-210 in Tours. Next his squadron was ordered to Meknes, Morocco. When France fell, Gary managed to join up with Polish troops sailing on a British cargo ship, the *Oakrest,* hoping to join de Gaulle in England. They sailed via Gibraltar to Glasgow, where he became part of the Free French air force and began flying bombing missions, destroying enemy aircraft. At least one hundred fifty missions were flown. Of his group of fifty French airmen, only Gary and two others survived to see the end of the war. From Glasgow he was transferred to French Equatorial Africa. One plane in which he was flying crashed in Nigeria, and another in Kumasi, on the way to Cairo. Both the navigator and the pilot were killed, but Gary survived. He contracted typhoid in Damascus, rejoined his squadron in the Sudan, got stranded in Egypt, got malaria, was sent to Libya for tests to see if he'd contracted leprosy since he'd fallen in love with a young girl who came down with the disease, and was sent away. At this point he'd been promoted to second lieutenant. In Damascus, suffering with typhoid, he lay near death for several weeks. The doctor and the Armenian nun who nursed him, believing that he had only a few hours to live and assuming he was Catholic, arranged for extreme unction to be administered. An orderly even placed a wooden coffin at the foot of his bed, in preparation for death. A friend later told him that he was hanging on to life the way a miser hung on to money. Of course, Gary explained, "I had a promise to keep. I had to return home, my hands full of victories, write *War and Peace* and become an ambassador of France"—to please his mother.

The uncut umbilical cord remained strong, and—as she'd managed to do throughout the war, through a liaison in Switzerland—his mother's buoying weekly letters continued to reach him in Damascus while he lay dying, just as they had in France, in England and in North Africa. He began to recover, though side effects like phlebitis, facial paralysis, gallbladder disease, purulent sores dogged him. When Gary was well enough to read the stack of his mother's letters that lay unopened on the bedside table, he quenched this filial thirst for the sound of his mother's voice. Strength and courage seeped from her words into his soul. These short, undated, weekly, sometimes daily missives usually began, *Dear Romouchka . . . have courage. Be brave. Be strong, I beg you. Your mother.* For the rest of his life, and in his memoir *Promises at Dawn,* he would contend that "the will, the vitality and the courage of my mother continued to flow into me and keep me alive."

Although his doctor had informed him that his fighting days were over for good, Romain hired an Egyptian taxi driver to impersonate him—RAF uniform and all—before the Cairo board that was to declare him fit. And did. Though weak and depleted, he began flying dangerous missions again. He rejoined his squadron in the eastern Mediterranean, bombed German submarines off the coast of Cyprus. Although destruction, confusion and chaos accelerated as the end of the war approached, his mother's letters continued faithfully to follow him via Switzerland to the eastern Mediterranean, where he flew fifteen dangerous missions. On one of these missions, both Gary—the navigator—and his friend Arnaud Langer—the pilot—were wounded, Gary in the belly and Arnaud in both eyes. Somehow, Gary and the crew were able to guide the blind pilot and the aircraft to a safe landing. When he was released from hospital once more, Gary rejoined the Lorraine Squadron of the Free French. While bombing Rommel's troops, he received a telegram informing him that he'd been awarded the Cross of the Liberation. The telegram was signed by Charles de Gaulle, who, many months later, after the liberation of France and war's end, personally, movingly, would pin the green and black ribbon onto Gary's uniform under the Arc de Triomphe.

Just before the liberation of France in 1944, Gary was parachuted into southern France to join the Resistance. Exalted to be on French soil, he decided it was time to try to reach his mother in Nice. After the Allies had landed in southern France, he was able to make his way by land to Toulon. In ten different ways, messages of his approach had been earmarked to be given to his mother— through the Maquis, by way of soldiers who were parachuting down in the Nice vicinity even before the landings. He didn't know if any of these messages would reach her to say that he was alive and that he was on his way home. As he approached, he became exhilarated by the sight of familiar Mediterranean pines and cypresses, olive and orange groves. Gary passed the debris of war along the road to Nice. He saw pocked roads, burned tanks. When he crossed the Var River, his heart was bursting because the landscape had become familiar. In preparation for the reunion, he pinned his medals across his black battle uniform with the captain's stripes sewn onto the sleeve. Proudly he displayed his Croix de Guerre, his Legion of Honor, his Cross of the Liberation. Then he cocked his hat at a rakish angle when he turned on the familiar street of the Hôtel-Pension Mermonts, run by his mother.

Gary described the last time he'd seen her. She'd taken his arm. Rather than dimming them, her newly acquired horn-rimmed glasses made her beautiful green eyes more vivid. Though she'd begun leaning on a walking stick, was suffering from eczema at her wrists, though her face was deeply lined, it had exuded unfaltering confidence except briefly when he'd warned her, "Not one pilot in ten will see the end of the war." She'd begun to tremble and weep, but had quickly regained her confident air, assuring him, "Nothing is going to happen to you," and added, "You may, perhaps, be wounded in the leg." He recalled that her eyes again were burning with confidence. It was then that she'd used her finger to make the sign of the cross over him. *"Blagoslavliayou tiebia!"* And as he approached the Hôtel-Pension Mermonts, bearing the scars of many war wounds, he acknowledged that she'd been right. He had been wounded but—as she'd promised—nothing had happened to him. He didn't know it yet, but before too many years his first novel, *A European Education,* would win the Prix des Critiques. Although he would not live to old age, Gary would write many more books. He would ascend the diplomatic ladder, becoming French consul general in Los Angeles and first secretary of the French delegation to the United Nations. Her words then, and her words in every one of the multitude of letters she'd written to him through the war, had been prophetic. He was—though wounded, yes—returning home to her intact, a sterling though as yet unknown future ahead of him.

When Romain entered the Hôtel-Pension Mermonts, he was greeted by strangers who only had the vaguest knowledge that, yes, a Russian woman had once run the place. They told him she'd been gone for a long time. His anxious inquiries to other sources brought forth the information that the Russian woman he was seeking had died many years before—at least three and a half years—quite early in the war, in fact. It took Romain a while to learn that, to be specific, she had died quite soon after he'd said his last goodbye to her and set out for England. Eventually, he put all the pieces together. Not only had his mother known that she didn't have much time to live when they'd said that goodbye, but she'd spent the last nights and days, as her life drained away, writing undated letters to him that were infused with encouragement. She'd written over two hundred and fifty letters, had slyly colluded with a friend in Switzerland who was under no circumstances to let Romain know that she had died. The instructions were that the friend would send them to her son at consistent intervals, which is exactly what the friend had done. Gary wrote, "She had known that I was still a weakling then, and that I would never be able to stand on my own feet and fight as befits a Frenchman unless she was there to give me her support; and she had made her plans accordingly . . . and so I had gone on receiving from my mother the strength and the courage I so greatly needed

Letter from Romain Gary's mother: *My dear, my beloved, Rromanchka! I give you my blessing, and I swear to you that your departure did not sadden me but gave me only joy. Be tough, be strong. Mama.*

to carry me through to the day of victory, when she had been dead for more than three and a half years. The umbilical cord had continued to function."

At about age five, Romain had traveled beside his mother by sleigh through the Russian countryside. As the actress Nina Borisovskaia, she was giving readings of Chekhov and Russian poetry to workers in factories and soldiers in their chilly winter barracks. Usually during every performance, a worker or a soldier would hoist the boy up onto his shoulders to see his mother's face—in full makeup, eyes highlighted in black, lips painted bright red—to hear her declaim with emotive invective, spellbinding both the audience and him. After the performance, he remembered snuggling against her in the freezing night, under layers of warm blankets that were pulled up to their noses, listening to the tinkle of the bells hanging from the horses' necks as the sleigh pulled them through the densely packed snow. Although he would later become fluent in Polish, French and English, it was the rich, evocative Russian language he and his mother spoke to each other in which she invoked her dream of his invincibility.

HUMAN KINDNESS

Before you know what kindness really is
You must lose things,
Feel the future dissolve in a moment
Like salt in a weakened broth.
What you held in your hand,
What you counted and carefully saved,
All this must go so you know
How desolate the landscape can be
Between the regions of kindness.
How you ride and ride
Thinking the bus will never stop,
The passengers eating maize and chicken
        will stare out the window forever.

Before you learn the tender gravity of kindness,
You must travel where the Indian in a white poncho
Lies dead by the side of the road.
You must see how this could be you
How he too was someone
Who journeyed through the night with plans
And the simple breath that kept him alive.

Before you know kindness as the deepest thing inside,
You must know sorrow as the other deepest thing.
You must wake up with sorrow.
You must speak to it till your voice
Catches the thread of all sorrows
And you see the size of the cloth.

Then it is only kindness that makes sense anymore,
Only kindness that ties your shoes
And sends you out into the day to mail letters and purchase bread
Only kindness that raises its head
From the crowd of the world to say
It is I you have been looking for,
And then goes with you everywhere
Like a shadow or a friend.

"KINDNESS"—*Naomi Shihab Nye*

Although there had been no anti-Semitic tradition in Italy as there had been in Germany and other parts of Europe, Jewish killings and deportations finally began in Italy in 1943. They started in Rome and moved north. In flight, Jews dispersed toward the north. Many Jews or opponents of Mussolini or the Fascist regime who were caught by the Gestapo were sent to prisoner-of-war camps north of the Apennines. The catch of Jews was small indeed because so many Jews and partisans and other opponents of Fascism had found hiding places in small villages and in the mountains.

One of these, protected by mountain people and villagers, was neither a Jew nor a partisan. He was in the British army and had

been smuggled into Italy to blow up an airport. The plan had failed
and he'd been captured by the Italian army. The soldier's name was
Eric Newby, and he returned to the mountains and forests of the
Apennines twelve years after war's end with his wife and two children, to find, visit and somehow thank the various men, women
and children who'd sheltered, fed and protected him for more than
a year after his escape in 1943 from a prisoner-of-war camp outside
the village of Pianura Pada, not far from the city of Parma. All who
had helped him, and those who had helped Jews and other "outlaws," had done so at the risk of their own lives.

Over the course of that year, separately and together, a human
lifeline had been spontaneously created that sustained Newby's
body and kept his spirit alive. As he wrote in *Love and Death in the
Apennines,* all help "was given freely at the time, out of kindness of
heart." The first link in his human lifeline was a tall Italian farmer
with a florid face, Signor Merli, who allowed Newby to spend the
first night after his escape hidden in his hayloft. He was impressed
by the farmer's large Roman nose. Although he'd managed to ac-
quire an Italian phrase book before escaping from the camp into
the countryside, Newby and Merli couldn't speak to each other.
Because Newby had a broken leg and because it was daylight and
dangerous, Merli hurriedly helped him up a steep, rickety ladder
into the hayloft. He gave him a bottle filled with fresh water and
left him. Suffering severe pain in the broken leg, Newby listened
to the sound of explosions in the foothills of the Apennines
that—he correctly assumed—were being made by the advancing
Germans.

When dark, accompanied by a heavy mist, had entirely fallen,
Newby was helped into the farmer's house and the farmer's small,
dark wife fed him pasta and salty cheese, which he washed down

with frothing purple wine. As he wolfed down the food, the farmer's two children studied his unusual uniform and boots. Then he was put to bed on feed sacks in the cowshed. In the morning, an Italian doctor came to look at his leg and arranged to have him taken to hospital. When Newby gestured goodbye to Signor Merli and his family, Signora Merli began to cry. He was taken by the dissident doctor to the Ospedale Peracchi near Fontanellato and hidden in a bed in the maternity ward. His helpers had agreed that if he didn't get his leg set—couldn't walk, couldn't run—he didn't stand a chance of escaping. Cheese, fruit, eggs, cigarettes and civilian clothes were brought to him by women and young girls who arrived out of nowhere on bicycles. Immediately he was visited in the hospital by a slim, blue-eyed young woman named Wanda, a Slovene from a place close to Ljubljana, who had lived in Italy with her father for a long time and obviously was connected to the dissidents who were helping him. She insisted that he learn Italian, which she would teach him. Neither could have imagined at that moment of meeting that they would be reunited after the war and would marry each other. The doctor set his leg in a plaster cast, and while the bone mended, Wanda's Italian lessons began.

When the Germans discovered Newby at the hospital, he was put under armed guards. After several days a note was left under his lunch plate: *Tonight, 22:00, if not, Germany tomorrow, 06:00. Go east 500 metri across fields until you reach a bigger street. Wait there! Don't worry about clothes and shoes.* That night, feigning diarrhea, he went back and forth to the bathroom. When the hallway was clear, he climbed down a drainpipe outside the toilet window and hobbled away per the instructions. Waiting at the crossroads was an old car that had the Red Cross symbol painted on its door. Inside sat the doctor who had already helped him, along with a schoolteacher, referred to as "Maestro," who happened to be Wanda's father. They drove Newby toward the large outlines of the Apennines, and after a night in the woods near the Po River, he was taken in hand by a large limping man with a scar along his nose. This was Signor Giovanni, who left him in an underground hole with a promise to return. The hole had recently been dug by the gnarled hands of Giovanni and his very old father. It was fortified with sacks and a few provisions that included a blanket, water, cheese, wine and a can into which he could evacuate. All night, rain fell on the makeshift roof and dripped through the airhole until—late the next day—the coast was clear and Giovanni and his father came to retrieve him.

His next shelter was two villages farther up, on a mountainside. It was a stone hut the size of a cowshed that he first saw illuminated by fierce lightning. It belonged to the Zanoni family. Fearing expulsion when Signor Zanoni told him he couldn't sleep in the hay, his heart sank. But then Zanoni announced that he could sleep in the house in a bed after he finished milking his cow. With relief, Newby was shortly brought there. Zanoni's house seemed more a cave than a house. The stones glowed red from hanging oil lamps. Zanoni, his wife, their three children and a small and wrinkled aunt who watched him constantly through thick glasses—six people in all—lived in this cavelike residence. Newby was fed potato gnocchi and given red wine to drink, then he was put into the warmest, softest bed in which he'd ever slept— before or since. The knitted vest they gave him smelled strongly of sheep. He fell asleep to the sound of crashing rain and woke to sounds of cows and hens in the yard below. It was September 1943, and the reward for denouncing a fugitive like himself or a Jew or a partisan had just risen to eighteen hundred lire, at a time when a thousand lire meant a comfortable life for a month. The sentence for aiding or abetting any one of these outlaws was execution.

Newby's next shelter was several hours by foot through the woods, higher in the mountains. His shelterers were a thin, erect farmer, Signor Luigi, who always wore a hat; his wife, Agata, who had a booming voice and was missing a tooth; their daughters, Rita, thin and dour, and Dolores, Amazonian and lusty; a plow-boy, Armando; and a ferocious dog named Nero. These mountain people spoke a mountain dialect. Despite the risk, the arrangement was that Newby would be fed and sheltered at Pian del Sotto—as the place was called—in exchange for field work. Since he would be working outside most of the day, a story would be circulated that he was deaf and dumb, a bombed-out fisherman originally from Genoa.

The next link in Newby's chain of helpers—albeit an accidental protector—was encountered after Newby had spent a sun-drenched autumn Sunday gathering mushrooms near a cliff that was about five or six thousand feet above the valley. He was lying on a spot of soft underbrush soaking up the afternoon heat and had let the lazy sounds of bees, insects, sheep bells and even a tolling church bell in the valley lull him to sleep. When he opened his eyes, a German officer—armed, in uniform—was towering above him. His name was Oberleutnant Frick. Flat on his back, Newby was frozen to the spot on which he lay. He was shirtless, bootless, sockless, weaponless. He thought about the choices available at that instant—murder, combat. One quick shove might send the German tumbling off the high cliff behind him. Or? Or? Or he could act the part of the Italian deaf-mute. However, he couldn't will himself into action, he simply lay where he was, frozen. He realized that the German was also frozen. After a decisive moment, rather than fight to the death, the two soldiers continued doing nothing, continued staring at each other. Then Newby noticed the butterfly net that Frick was toting and the moment of jeopardy dissolved and they began to converse.

This German was a professor of entomology from Göttingen who was in Italy lecturing on Renaissance painting and architecture to soldiers who were engaged in destroying these very things. Newby and Frick drank a beer from Munich together. They discussed the war, the impending German defeat. Before leaving Frick told him, "Do not be afraid. I will not tell anyone that I have met you. I am anxious to collect specimens . . . specimens with wings." Strange as it felt, Newby shook the hand that was offered and—still seated, agape—watched Frick, the sworn enemy, take off across a field, his net lunging at a butterfly unseen to him.

Forced by the tightening German noose to move again, Newby next met Abramo, a huge man with mottled skin and a viselike handshake, a shepherd who lived even higher in the mountains to the west of Pian del Sotto, among gray cloudbanks, with flocks of black and dun-colored sheep and dogs in an area peppered with dwarf beech trees. Abramo's hut smelled of sheep, was less than ten feet square. Abramo gave Newby grappa to drink, polenta, hare stew flavored with mushrooms, herbs and giblet gravy to eat. The stay here lasted only a few days. Next—because it was becoming too dangerous for him to be sheltered in anyone's house at all, six male members of the community built a secret house for him. A lean man with a sharp nose named Francesco was in charge. A very old man named Bartolomeo and four others, including Francesco's boy Pierino, and a mule climbed very high into the mountains together and worked all day. When the outside of the makeshift house/cave was finished, the helpers stacked wood inside and created a chimney in the cliff wall. Late in the day, the wives of the men appeared at the building site loaded down with backpacks filled with cheese and rice, bread, salt and acorn coffee purchased at exorbitant prices—which none could afford—on the black market. And of course they'd brought wine. A password—"Brindisi"—was agreed upon. Gathering their tools, the Italians wished him luck and led the donkey down the mountainside, disappearing quickly.

Entirely alone, Newby undraped the sacking that covered the entrance. He climbed behind the tangled beech tree roots and stepped inside his cave home. Once inside he let the sacking fall back behind the roots, rendering the door to his refuge entirely invisible. While inside he could hear the hoot of forest owls through the long, lonely winter months he spent based at this refuge in solitude except for visits from the children or grandmothers of his shelterers, bringing him food—eggs, sausage, but more often bread, milk and soup. "Almost always they came when it was just growing light; but I was always awake. . . . Then they would hand me the pot—and after I had handed back the pot, I would receive words of encouragement, and usually, in answer to my question, they would say that there was *niente di nuovo*—no news. This meant in the *comune* rather than the world, although they sometimes would add—dabbing their eyes—that there was still no news of the boys in Russia, whose grandmothers some of them were, and then they would go back down the hill, very black and respectable, with the pot concealed in a black bag made of American cloth."

So he remained when fierce rain, then blizzards, came to the mountains, when bombs began to fall on Genoa. One day the son of one of the protectors arrived in an anxious state. He told

Newby that he must leave in less than an hour, that the *milizia* was coming for him that very night. He took rice and other supplies and was guided to a rendezvous with a boy—Alfredo, slim, shy, whose lips were blue from cold—who led him safely around frozen waterfalls, iced gorges, through a night of wailing winds, to the hut of a family of charcoal burners whose faces were dusted black from charcoal. There he was given bracing grappa and the warmth of a hot fire. From this refuge he was led by a boy to a barn where an almost blind man, Amadeo, awaited them, as well as a small girl carrying a crock of hot soup. While Newby ate, Amadeo told him, "I, too, will give you food and shelter for as long as you wish to stay here."

The chain of human kindness held firm during his time in the mountains.

I met Ruth Jacobsen on the last day in December on Long Island, where she lives. We sat together in her study decorated with her artwork, and she softly spoke with me. The trace of an accent was still evident in her speech. She showed me many of the collages she'd made using photographs from her childhood. I was struck that, although over fifty years had passed, the little German girl in the photos still looked eerily like the woman sitting three feet away from me. If I'd met Ruth in a room full of people after seeing her childhood photographs, I would have still been able to pick Ruth out of the crowd—her blue eyes, her round cheeks were the same. She was in possession of these family photo albums because through the war a neighbor had hidden and preserved them even though to harbor Jewish property was a crime punishable by death or imprisonment. But this man—a Dutch-

Collage by Ruth Jacobsen.

man named Cees van Bart—had done so anyway. After the war he returned them to Ruth, who put the photo albums away because she was determined to forget the past. She succeeded in burying and blurring these memories for quite some time.

She brought them with her when she emigrated to the United States in 1953, and still didn't look at these photographs for forty years; her past became even vaguer. She became an artist and created books of collages. But then as she explained, "One day I found the courage to pick up the albums. My fear had always been that I would break down and become hysterical at seeing my parents' images again. Finally I was able to put aside the fears I had felt for so many years and look at the photos. The photographs evoked feelings I could only express in collage form. I needed to move the photographs out of the albums and into my life. I used the original photographs, as well as letters, other images and acrylic paints, to create collages. In the process of working with them, more and more of the past came back. I began to remember . . ."

Ruth was born in Frankenberg, Germany. Her parents owned the local shoe store but moved the family to Düsseldorf when Hitler came to power and they were forced to sell their store. On the infamous Kristallnacht—the Night of Broken Glass, November 9, 1938—her parents and seven-year-old Ruth had been warned of roundups of Jews, so they walked around Düsseldorf through the night until morning. "As we walked we saw glass, furniture and even people being thrown out of windows. I remem-

Interior of the Fasanenstrasse Synagogue in Berlin after its destruction on Kristallnacht, 1938.

ber the sound of crashing objects and a thick blanket of fear sur-rounding us." A short time later, wearing two layers of clothing, carrying a doll named Ellen, she and her parents boarded a train. They got off the train in Utrecht, a city across the border in the Netherlands. Here they were met by the Baroness van Tuyll van Serooskerken (whose husband was a friend of Ruth's father) in a chauffeur-driven limousine. They were driven to Oud Zuylen on the Vecht River. At first they lived in the baron's fourteenth-century castle, then they were moved into a small furnished house nearby, where marigolds grew in the garden. Ruth entered the lo-cal school, quickly learned Dutch and made friends. At the time the fad among the girls her age was to wear alphabet pins. Her "R" glowed in the dark, it was phosphorescent. She wore it on her coat proudly. On May 10, 1940, the Germans attacked Holland. Ruth was eight.

Ruth vividly recollects the distinctive sound of her mother's voice: "One night many years after she died, I heard my mother's voice I was sleeping when I heard her say, 'Ruth.' I answered, 'Yes?' which woke me up. Her voice seemed so close and clear that it sounded as if she was right next to me. I got out of bed and looked for her but there was no one there." By 1942, Jews in German-occupied Holland were being hunted by the Nazis. Clasping her doll Ellen, Ruth was taken with her mother and father by Cees van Bart, who had become a member of the Dutch Resistance, to a house where they were hidden. When that place became unsafe, the Resistance moved them to another hiding place. Eventually, because of the difficulty of finding safe houses, Ruth's parents went to one hiding place and she was sent to another. Be-cause she had blue eyes and spoke good Dutch, she was allowed to play outside with other children while her parents were forced to remain indoors. Since the name Ruth sounded too Jewish, she was told to choose another name. She chose a typical Dutch name—Truusje. She was passed from stranger to stranger, was taken on trains, brought into strange homes. In one hiding place, she helped out by taking a goat to a meadow at dawn. In another, she cared for pet rabbits. In yet another, she faced a dreamy lake on which sailboats tacked into the wind. The strangers were called *oom*—uncle—and *tante*—aunt. At one point, she was hidden with a family that had six children. Hidden with her was a pale, nervous Jewish boy who played chess by himself all day. This boy's arms and hands were covered with eczema.

The various hiding places were in Amsterdam and also in small towns in the south of Holland. At war's end, Ruth and her parents ended up in separate hiding places in the south of Holland around Maastricht. She was thirteen years old. She remembers: "At last the war was over. Armies no longer marched through our streets. Soldiers no longer went to the front. People tried to return to normal lives, but my parents never could. The years of hiding had damaged them somehow, and peace didn't end their torment." She went to live with her parents in an abandoned house and returned to school. It was a Catholic elementary school, since the southern part of Holland is largely Catholic. At this school she was treated kindly by the nuns. Although Europe had begun the process of rebuilding, her parents were unable to recover their equilibrium. Ruth watched her mother slip into deep depression. "To her, life was not worth living anymore. I made a great effort to hold her hand despite my terror that I would fall into her depression by just touching her." After an overdose of sleeping pills her mother was put into a mental hospital and was given shock treatments. None of the treatments that were tried helped. Eventually, one of her mother's many suicide attempts succeeded. "I was not allowed to go to the burial and there was no funeral service. In the Jewish religion a person who commits suicide is buried without rituals."

In winter of 1953, sponsored by distant relatives, Ruth sailed alone from Rotterdam for New York. Ten days later, at night, she and other passengers stood on the deck as the ship approached land. "I saw what looked like a small brightly lit city, with a gigantic Ferris wheel glittering in the night. I was told this was Coney Island. It was America welcoming me to start a new life." In spring of 1954, her father also committed suicide. Ruth believes that "the Nazis had killed them as surely as if they had died in a camp." In 1959, she returned to Europe for the first time and visited the cemetery in southern Holland where her parents were buried. She also visited some of the people who'd helped to hide her, as well as several of the houses in which she'd been hidden. "Most of the *ooms* and *tantes* who risked their lives to hide me or help me were lost to me as soon as I left their homes. But I was able to contact a few of my rescuers after the war. I would periodically return to Holland to visit Cees van Bart, Tante Marie and Sister Calasancta, a Catholic nun."

She described her first visit back: "On my first visit, Cees brought me to the house my family had gone to our first night of hiding. I did not recognize the house and he did not tell me where we were. When we went up to the second floor and looked out the window, I knew. It was the same window through which I had watched my friends playing while I was in hiding. I became agitated and came down with a violent attack of diarrhea. We left and didn't come back. Cees had no idea I would react that way."

When Ruth asked Cees how he'd found the courage to risk his life to help her family, he replied, "I didn't think about it. I just did what was right in the situation." She explained to me that she didn't discover until many years after Cees had died that, because of his Underground work helping Jews and committing sabotage against the Germans, he too had been forced to go into hiding at various times, had narrowly escaped death. During the remainder of her first visit and on subsequent trips, Cees rarely mentioned the war again.

Ruth recalls a woman she'd met on a bus in Utrecht when she was nine years old and Jews had just been ordered to wear a yellow Star of David sewn onto their coats. She was on a bus on her way to school. "A group of boys from the Dutch Hitler Youth got into the bus. When they saw my yellow star, they demanded my seat even though the bus was half-empty. Everybody looked uncomfortable but no one dared to interfere. The boys were rough and rowdy and felt their power. I remained seated, immobilized with fear, not comprehending the fury they directed to me. One of the passengers motioned to me. I left my seat and went to her. Without a word she pointed to her lap where I was to sit for the rest of the trip." Of course, later, there was no way to find this woman to thank. She'd been one—of many—strangers who'd risked all to help a small girl with blue eyes and round cheeks.

Before the war Mr. Jablonsky was the secondary-school math teacher in the small city of Kaunas, Lithuania. He was a friendly man but was a strict teacher who expected obedience and hard work from his pupils. He sported a dour gray mustache, taught teenagers in that city. Kaunas is a place of church spires and chestnut trees. It's also known as Kovno and is surrounded by crumbling old, once strategic forts built by a Russian czar. One of Mr. Jablonsky's students was a tall, lean boy with bright blue eyes and dirty blond hair whose father was a champion chess player from Berlin. His mother was Russian, from Moscow, a well-known, talented violinist whose stage name was Vera Shore. The boy's name was Kuki Kopelman. He was much loved by the Kaunas Jewish community because of his many talents—tap dancing, violin playing, chess playing—and his abundant charm. Kuki was thought of as a prodigy. A rumor had gone around Kovno that he had been spotted by a scout and invited to Hollywood.

Kuki was in his early teens in 1941 when Germany occupied Lithuania. Once in Kovno, the Germans set up a Jewish ghetto in a dilapidated neighborhood across the Vilijampole Bridge, known as Vilijampole but called Slabodke by the thirty thousand Jews who were squeezed inside, the Kopelman family among them. A gate was erected, sharp barbed wire was strung between the Vilija River and Krisciukaicio Street in lieu of a wall. In the early days of the Slabodke ghetto, the weekly food ration per person was a few potatoes, seven hundred grams of bread, one hundred twenty-five grams of horsemeat, one hundred twenty-two grams of flour, fifty grams of salt and seventy-five grams of ersatz coffee. Quickly hunger began to gnaw at and preoccupy the inhabitants.

Another student of Mr. Jablonsky, whose parents happened also to be friendly with Kuki's parents, was Solly Genkind—who, after the war, when he'd gone to Palestine to fight for Israeli independence, would rename himself Solly Ganor and whom I would later meet in California and come to know. Solly only casually knew Kuki before the war, but in the ghetto, he and Kuki forged a deep friendship that would feed and nurture his starved spirit while enduring the living hell of ghetto life.

Solly was thirteen in 1941, had a sensual face, very dark hair and shining, dark eyes. Tragedy had already affected his family; he had seen death close up several times. His older brother Herman and several relatives had already disappeared and were probably dead. His extended family of nine lived in the ghetto in a small wooden two-room apartment on Gimbuto Street—no toilet, no running water. To pass the long nights, he began to read *War and Peace* and other books he could get his hands on. He could read German and Lithuanian, also Yiddish and Russian. When he could find them, he enjoyed reading English and American books that had been translated into Russian or German. When we spoke, he explained to me that he considered his passion for reading books to have helped him forget how hungry he was while he was in the ghetto.

Sometimes on a short break from the backbreaking work gang to which he was assigned—to try to block out the all-pervasive ugliness around him—Solly would try to remember the beauty of the Lithuanian countryside, the River Nemunas fed by pure white snow from Russia in which he used to swim in summer. He'd close his eyes, picture the river and the view of chestnut trees. He explained to me that he remembers thinking to himself at such moments, "O God! If you will only make this nightmare go away, I will bless your wondrous creation every day of my life. I will kiss every tree and praise every flower. I will spend my life serving the poor. I'll help every stray dog and cat that crosses my path. Please, God . . ."

One morning both Solly and Kuki were not chosen for a work brigade. Having a free morning, Kuki invited Solly up to the attic room above the small apartment his family shared with another couple. Kuki often used the attic as a hiding place when the Germans would terrorize people while making their searches for gold and other valuables. Solly was thrilled by the books Kuki had managed to hide, especially Jules Verne because he was mad about Captain Nemo. The boys quickly established their mutual love of books. Solly was already warming to Kuki and confided in him by relating a dream he often had in which it was he, Solly, not Noah, who escorted pairs of animals onto the ark. Kuki interpreted the dream in an amusing way, made Solly laugh. By the end of that first day, the boys had begun to call their beloved books "our alligators, snakes and hyenas." In the intimacy of the hiding place, Solly also confessed to Kuki that he was in love with Lena Greenblatt, who had an appealing face and lived on Linkovos Street with her mother. Solly confided that he'd even kissed her on the lips.

After that, they got together whenever they could. Solly brought Kuki to Linkovos Street to meet Lena. Lena was suffering greatly because her father had recently been taken up to one of the abandoned forts by the Germans with about five hundred others from the ghetto. He had never returned. Seeing Lena's sad countenance, Kuki performed a comic tap dance that included tumbling in a cartwheel and further hijinks until he had Lena and Solly laughing so hard their sides hurt. When Kuki was finished, Lena's cheeks were rosy and she was actually still laughing. Solly saw that Lena had quickly—as he had—warmed to Kuki. Then, as Solly watched, Kuki planted a kiss above Lena's pert nose. Before they left she called them "you two clowns" and kissed them both. Solly felt a fierce fork of jealousy stab him as Kuki and he walked away. But a few days later, when Kuki confessed that he'd also fallen in love with Lena, the prongs of jealousy were much less piercing because the delightful bond of friendship had widened to include Lena.

In fall 1941, two thousand more inhabitants of the ghetto were murdered by German soldiers with the willing help of local Lithuanians. Some of these people were burned to death, others shot and buried in mass graves that the Jews themselves had been forced to dig. Whenever possible Lena, Kuki and Solly met in a second hiding place belonging to a kind old man with snow-white hair named Chaim who had owned a bookshop before the war and had smuggled an entire attic full of books into the ghetto with him. He made them welcome in his attic. This cluttered attic was filled with piles of books that Chaim generously shared with the three friends. Together, the three of them read *Three Comrades* by Erich Maria Remarque, a book about a romantic friendship between two men and a woman. Though the woman's life ends in tragedy, the triangular friendship in the novel became the touchstone for their intensifying friendship. They came to consider themselves "three comrades" too. In this attic, Chaim occasionally would lecture the triumvirate on great books and read to them from Stefan Zweig, Franz Kafka, Thomas Mann and others. Chaim had managed to bring an old gramophone with him into the ghetto and would play classical music for the young people. Fearing for his precious books, Chaim wouldn't allow any books to be removed from the attic at first. But after he knew the three comrades better, he allowed each of them to borrow books on the condition that they would be returned. Chaim described the Russian defeat of Napoleon in great detail and infused a small whiff of hope into all three hearts when he predicted that the Germans would meet with a similar, resounding defeat, just as Napoleon had.

When another five hundred inhabitants of the ghetto were sent to their deaths, the entire ghetto was stunned. Lena's face had become the face of a wraith. Solly remembers that at that point she admitted to them, "I don't want to die. Death is horrible. . . . I feel it coming like a faceless evil, creeping up on us from the unknown. I wish I could be a believer. But all I see is a bottomless black pit." Solly too felt hot anger toward God. He remembers wanting to shout, "Hey, God! Wake up there! Look what they are doing to your chosen people. They are murdering us, and you do nothing! Where are you? God of Abraham and Isaac, where are you?" But, not to depress Lena further, he didn't say any of this out loud to his friends. Instead, with pretended bravado, he and Kuki tried to comfort Lena as much as they could. Chaim offered the solace of the attic and of beautiful music by playing his favorite piece, Beethoven's Fifth Symphony, for them. Chaim commented on the sensation of peace albeit temporary that music brought to the attic: "It's the only art form in which a group of human beings can achieve almost total unison." Chaim was right. Fraught and anxious as the three friends were, they felt some peace when listening—sometimes to Grieg, sometimes to Rimsky-Korsakov's *Schéhérazade* or Tchaikovsky's *Nutcracker*.

One day it was decreed that the entire ghetto was to assemble at Demokratu Square at six in the morning on October 28. The three friends feared another mass liquidation that would no doubt include all of them and their remaining families. Kuki angrily asked Chaim, "How have we come to this? How could we have provoked the wrath and hatred of all of Europe?" Chaim offered his opinion with similar anger. "They really do hate us. Passionately and mercilessly. And it stems from the fact that endless generations of Christians were brainwashed to hate us by the Christian churches."

Half a century later, while lunching at an Indian restaurant in Santa Monica, California, with Solly and his wife, Pola, Solly described to me how, once they'd begun to spend time together, his closeness with Lena and Kuki had deepened. When he spoke of this long-ago friendship, he gave the impression that the memory of the friendship still affected him. I'd quickly warmed and felt a rapport with Solly when we met. It seemed as if his capacity for attracting friendship had not diminished. He described how on that Sunday after the decree was posted, he went with Kuki to see Lena. "She was waiting for us on the doorstep, and without a word we all put our arms around each other. We stood and clung together in silence for quite a while. At that moment, words were simply meaningless. We knew that we might soon be running through a hail of bullets at the Ninth Fort. How could we possibly console each other? Kuki began crying first and we soon joined him. We felt tenderness for each other that only the approach of death could fully expose. There were so many things yet to be done, books to read, movies to watch, marriage, children, a world to explore . . . I will always remember the quiet sorrow on Lena's face when we said goodbye, how she stood on the steps in the twilight, watching us go."

The morning of the giant selection—October 28, 1941—is described by Solly like this: "The streets were covered with an early morning frost, and mist shrouded the fields. It was going to be a cold day. I pulled the flaps of my leather hat down to protect my ears. Hundreds of people were emerging from the houses all around us. In the semidarkness they looked like gray ghosts. Some carried candles, which cast an eerie light on their faces. Many were carrying small children in their arms, or pushing baby carriages through the sandy streets. Some supported their elderly parents; others carried invalids on stretchers. I began to hear a strange humming sound. When I listened closer, I realized that many were reciting psalms."

Twenty-eight thousand Jewish people were assembled in Demokratu Square, surrounded by machine guns manned by already drunk Lithuanians and Germans that day. Systematically, Rauca, the *Kommandant* of the ghetto, and the members of the Gestapo screened individuals, directing them singularly to the right or to the left, irrespective of family separations. Then they marched the designated ones away, as divided families howled. Solly recollects that his heart flailed wildly, he felt death's cold breath on his neck. While waiting, Solly scanned the crowd for a glimpse of his special friends but saw neither. The selection lasted the entire day and those not selected were sent home. This included Solly and his family. Everyone hoped against hope that the others would be resettled in a smaller ghetto nearby but realized it wasn't true when at dawn the following morning, the entire ghetto was able to view a never-ending column of humans moving slowly up the road along the hillside toward the Ninth Fort.

Solly described this indelible scene: "It wasn't as gory as many scenes I had witnessed, yet it was a thousand times worse. In my imagination I could see those unfortunate thousands being shoved into huge graves, layer upon layer of the dead being covered with freshly dug earth. Driven by an inexplicable force, we threw on our coats, and together with thousands of others we rushed to the ghetto fence. Armed Lithuanians lined both sides of the road as

Kaunas (Kovno), Lithuania, Jews assembled for a mass execution.

far as the eye could see. . . . It is impossible to describe the cries of
people from both sides of the fence as they recognized friends and
relatives, sometimes parents, brothers and sisters. How could
the heart take it in without breaking to pieces? How could the
mind remain sane? I kept trying to see if I recognized anyone on
the other side. The numbers were so great that the death march
lasted from dawn until noon. But we weren't able to bear it so
long and stumbled away, shocked to the bone."

Solly returned with his family to their rooms. He recalls getting in bed with his clothing on, and falling into a sickened sleep.
For two days the faraway sound of machine-gun fire tormented
those left alive in the ghetto. Later, when the survivors were able to
reconstruct the event, they tabulated that ten thousand people had
been made to march up to the Ninth Fort and were murdered

there. When the sound of the machine guns stopped, Solly tried unsuccessfully to locate Lena and Kuki. He found Chaim, who was in shock because his family had been taken, and he'd been wounded when he'd buried himself under a pile of hundreds of his beloved books and the Germans had sprayed the books with bullets. A bullet had grazed him. He was feeling terribly guilty, spoke to Solly as if he were a ghost, mused that he should have gone with them instead of hiding. Perhaps he could have saved them. After that, Chaim was distraught and listless. Even though Solly brought him bits of food, it was as if he was starving himself to death. Solly explains that he too was guilt-ridden but at the same time was convinced that his turn to die would surely come soon. Afterward, at night he'd throw himself into a book as deeply as he could to escape the overwhelming feelings that riddled him. He read by the dim light of bits of candle that his sister salvaged for him.

One evening when visiting Chaim, Solly heard the sound of a knuckle tapping glass. This sound caused his heart to gallop because this was the unmistakable signal only Kuki and he knew—three consecutive taps. He hurried outside. He smelled a terrible smell first, then—silhouetted in the milky moonlight, wearing a strange sheepskin hat and oversized overcoat, returned from the dead—he saw the pinched face of Kuki Kopelman. Seeing each other, they sat on the steps beside the house and wept bitterly. Aware of the cold, Solly pulled Kuki toward the door. "No one must see me," Kuki said. "If the Germans find out that I escaped, they'll come after me. No one must know. Not even my parents!"

Chaim and Solly heated up water and scrubbed Kuki as best they could, trying without success to eradicate the disgusting smell. Chaim gave him old clothes, told them both to try to sleep. Kuki sat in a crouch, rolling back and forth, his hands gripping each other. Solly remembers his countenance, the lean, rocking body: "As if he were trying to force an evil spirit out of his body, he began telling Chaim and me his story in a strange, low voice. It didn't sound like him at all." Even now, sixty years later, when Solly recalls the scene and story that Kuki told him, his eyes glaze with a frightening sheen that reminds me that, compassion aside, I am and will always remain an outsider to these experiences. With Solly as with every survivor I've spoken with, adding to the immense loss and loneliness each experienced and continues to experience, there is a permanent separation from anyone who didn't experience these times.

When speaking about this event, Solly's own voice is tightly coiled like a snail. The tightness never abates, from beginning to end of the telling that begins with Kuki's arrival at Chaim's: "After about ten minutes Kuki began to speak in that odd voice." Solly remembers his friend Kuki's words with minute and precise detail. Here is what Solly wrote about this exchange in his autobiography, *Light One Candle*:

In the beginning I tried to find my parents but it was an impossible task. A gasp seemed to go from the crowd, and I turned to see a group of German officers enter the square. Rauca had come. The selection was about to begin and the guards were forcing us into the nearest groups. Finally my eyes fell on a familiar face. I couldn't believe it. Right in front of me stood Lena and her family. At the same time, Lena turned her head and gasped in disbelief, "Kuki, oh Kuki! You're here," she cried out and started to weep.

It had become terribly clear that the side to the right was the bad side, and in our column most of the people were sent to the right. As we approached, Rauca just kept his stick extended to the right. We were condemned to death. When Rauca saw Lena he suddenly stopped our row, he signaled her out and told her to move to the left. "Du bist viel zu schön zum sterben," *he said. But Lena shook her head proudly and told him that she would share her family's fate.* "Very well," *he said, annoyed, and waved her away.*

After we were selected by Rauca, we were surrounded by dozens of German and Lithuanian policemen. Cursing and shouting obscenities at us, they herded us toward the small ghetto at a run. People who were too sick or old to keep up were beaten and trampled before our eyes. As soon as we arrived in the small ghetto the guards let us loose and everybody rushed to claim an empty house. "They're not taking us to the fort. They're not taking us to the fort!" *people began saying to each other. A spark of hope was rekindled in our hearts. Perhaps they really were only going to divide the population.*

Lena lay next to me and I could feel her trembling from fear and cold. After a while she whispered and asked if I was awake. I tried to quiet her and keep her warm, but she wanted to talk. "Kuki, what's going to happen to us? They're going to kill us tomorrow aren't they?" *I told her I didn't know.* "There are so many people here," *I said,* "I don't think they can kill so many people at once." *There was nowhere to run. All we could do was wait for the Germans to come. Just before they reached us, I felt almost resigned. But when they kicked in the outer door my calm completely shattered, we huddled together quaking with fear, and a strange odor suddenly filled the room. It was pure fear, the odor of death. Finally they burst into our room like a bunch of wild beasts, screaming orders. The hourglass was empty. I grabbed Lena by the arm and we ducked through a hail of blows out to the street. They were counting people off into groups of a hundred and when our turn came Lena and I were separated from her family and sent with another group.*

The road to the fort was uphill all the way and a difficult climb. Lena continued to cling to me, crying pitifully for her mother. In spite of the cold I was soon wet with perspiration. In front of us a long snake of people wound up the hill as far as the eye could see. Taking advantage of the confusion I began falling back, dragging Lena with me. I don't know why I did it. I knew that escape was impossible but I wanted to postpone death as long as I could. Lena's strength seemed to have left her completely and she could barely walk. I looked around trying to spot a familiar face but there were only strangers. Then I found a familiar face. It was my old math teacher, Jablonsky. He was a skeleton compared to what he used to be, but his gray mustache hadn't changed. He was breathing heavily as he struggled to keep up. I called out to him.

It was almost evening when we reached the fort. The walls were old and thick, with small barred windows. Lena was sobbing and trying to pray as they rose up in front of us. I was in turmoil. The deepest, most intrinsic, most pervasive instinct in us is the instinct for survival. No matter what poets say, when it comes to dying, everything else is forgotten. I heard Jablonsky say, "Don't cry, children. Let's not give them the satisfaction." German and Lithuanian guards stood at the entrance with large dogs straining at their leashes, barking and snarling furiously. We were pushed through the gates. A young German officer addressed us, "In spite of all the ridiculous rumors, you're going to be transported to working camps in the east. You will shower and then be issued working clothes. Undress and leave your clothing here." He spoke in civil tones, and in spite of all we knew about this death factory, he almost sounded convincing. But no one moved, no one seemed able to move a muscle. The officer calmly walked up to an elderly man who was standing near the front, drew his Luger and shot him in the face. When he fell to the ground his head opened up and his brains poured out into the mud. *Suddenly everyone was undressing. Finally we all stood naked, covering our private parts with our hands and shivering in the cold.*

Lena looked so terribly thin standing naked next to me. She was terribly ashamed to stand among naked men. I tried to say something comforting but my teeth were chattering uncontrollably. I wanted to say something meaningful to her. But what could I say? I was as terrified as she. At that moment I would have sold my soul to be able to die peacefully in bed between clean white sheets. On the officer's signal the Germans and Lithuanians launched themselves at us. "Run, run, you Jew swine," they shouted, lashing out at us with sticks and rifle butts, their dogs attacking the slow-moving ones, tearing pieces of flesh from their legs and buttocks. We started running in a wild panic with the guards and dogs after us. It was strange to see steam rising from all those bodies as they herded us along the wall of the fort. Then as we rounded a corner we saw dozens and dozens of machine guns mounted around an open field. They were firing long bursts into a huge pit. A mass of stampeding naked bodies crushed around me, encircling me like a straightjacket.

Lithuanians and Germans with rolled-up sleeves and red faces were loading and firing into the mob. You could see the yellow flashes from the barrels and a veil of blue smoke drifting over the field. There were hoarse shouts and women's screams—shrill—and children and babies crying and barking dogs. It stank of sweat and urine and excrement as terrified bodies just . . . let go. I saw one bearded man standing by the pit, shaking his fists at the sky and screaming, "Jews! There is no God!" He looked a lot like my old rabbi. Blood was streaming down him and they kept shooting at him but he kept standing there, screaming at the sky. We were right in front of the guns. Bullets were buzzing around me like angry bees but all I felt was the crush of the mob behind me. Then I felt myself falling with Lena still clinging to my arm. She was gripping me with a terrible force. There was a look of horror in her eyes and she was trying to say something. But only a croaking came from her lips. A gaping hole appeared in her throat and a stream of blood gushed out over her breast. Then I felt a weight fall on my head, knocking me into merciful oblivion.

I had that terrible nightmare again. Usually in the dream I would be lying in my crib and a huge striped tomcat was sitting on my chest, staring into my eyes. He was so heavy, I couldn't breathe. I was suffocating. Then my mother would appear and chase the cat away. I could breathe again. I had this nightmare many times in my childhood, but this time Mother wouldn't come. I was gasping for air and she wouldn't come. I knew that this time I would have to rescue myself or choke to death. I willed myself awake but even before I was fully awake I realized that I didn't really want to wake up. I tried to suck in some air but there wasn't any. Something enormously heavy was pressing down on my head, pushing my face into something soft and cold. The reality was that I was buried alive. I heaved and struggled but I was twisted in an awkward position and I felt like I had no strength at all. And yet, somehow, I managed a gulp of air. Cool, glorious air.

I realized that I was wedged in among several bodies. My head was resting on what was obviously a woman's large, cold, dead breast. I thought I would lose my sanity. I started struggling wildly. The body above shifted slightly, and suddenly my right arm was free. I twisted my neck, peering around and trying to see in the darkness. That's when I saw the stars. I dared not believe my senses and closed my eyes. When I opened them again, there they were, stars in the sky. It was the most beautiful, most moving sight . . . I was sure I was hallucinating. It must be night, for I can see the stars. The grave is open, but why? Then I remembered that it was almost evening when they shot us. They probably didn't have enough time to cover the pit before it got dark. Am I the *only one alive? Why was I chosen to lie here and wait until they bury me alive?*

It dawned on me that the body pinning me down must be alive as well because it was still warm. I started pushing at it with all my strength and screaming, "Are you alive? Can you hear me?" Finally he stirred and groaned. "Where am I? What is happening?" It was Jablonsky. He had been behind me when we were chased to the pit. He must have shielded me from the machine guns. I shouted at him, begging him to answer me. Finally he responded. "Kuki? Kuki? Is that you? Why are we still alive?" "Mr. Jablonsky, can you move at all? You're on top of me and I can't breathe. I'm not even wounded." I felt a slight movement. "I can't. I can't. I can't move anything." After another moment he said quietly, "Kuki, if you are not wounded, you must get away. You must go back. You must warn them. It is indecent to die like this. You must do this, Kuki. You must try to come out from under me," he insisted and I felt him strain his muscles to try to move. I began pushing and heaving with all my strength but to no avail. I lay back, trying to gather my strength again, both of us panting. Then suddenly there was a heave from below, as if the ground itself was shifting and somewhere beneath us a man screamed. Then it stopped. I felt Jablonsky's body slide off a little to the side. I began groping in the darkness and felt someone's head. The face was cold and clammy, and it had long hair. It was a woman's corpse and I hoped to God that it wasn't Lena. I pulled with all my strength and heard a snapping sound, as if the head was going to come off in my hand. I was filled with revulsion. . . .

When Solly recounts Kuki's description, he comments that when Kuki described the woman's corpse he became nauseous and began to vomit repeatedly and that Chaim went deathly white.

In his writing, he continues his description of what Kuki had told him:

I struggled until I was able to pull my body clear. Millions of stars were looking down on me. It was freezing cold. I might as well lie down and freeze to death and have it over with. Then I heard Jablonsky's voice again as if it were inside my own head. "Kuki. Go to the place we undressed. Get some warm clothing. You must make it back to the ghetto to warn them. You must bear witness. You must go, dear child." He sounded much weaker now. "I'll never make it," I cried. "They will catch me and kill me." "Hush, hush. They know that the dead don't walk out of the gate so what is there to watch? At least if they catch you, you'll die quickly."

I was weeping but Jablonsky wouldn't let me alone. "You must do one more thing. Before you leave, you must kill me. I know what I ask of you is a terrible thing, but please, Kuki. Please don't let them bury me alive." I begged him not to ask this of me, but he kept saying, "You must, Kuki, you must." I began grasping for straws. How was I to do this? I asked. With my bare hands? He spoke in a reasonable tone, as if this were an ordinary rational conversation. "Now what you must do is take the body above me and cover my face with it. You must press down hard. I won't last long." He was silent for a moment. "I'm ready to die now," he said then. "Goodbye, dear boy, and good luck." It went against every instinct in me but how could I refuse him? How could I leave him to suffer that terrible death? In the end I did what he asked me to do. It was a child's body I smothered him with.

Again I thought about just lying back and letting the cold finish me off. But now the cold was making me quake. I crept toward the wall where we had undressed, listening for guards. Nothing moved. I was es-

pecially afraid those dogs might come after me. But there were not even any dogs. I realized that unless I found some clothes soon I would pass out from the cold, and forced myself to run the last few hundred meters to the yard. Fortunately, the pile was still there. By the time I reached it my teeth were chattering uncontrollably. Most of the clothing I found belonged to grown-ups and was too big for me but I found warm underwear, a suit and a coat with a sheepskin lining. I padded the boots with several pair of socks. I discovered other treasures. In the pocket of the coat was a piece of bread. I didn't even bother to chew it; I just swallowed it whole. It occurred to me that there might be other food in other pockets. Luck was with me. I found more bread, margarine and a small jar of jam. A piece of sausage. I divided the food in two portions and ate half, hiding in the pile of clothing in case a guard turned up. But there was absolute stillness, as if I was the last man left alive on this cursed planet.

Suddenly overwhelmed with self-pity, I began to cry and cry and just couldn't stop. The distant barking of a dog brought me back to my senses. The Germans and Lithuanians might be back soon. I had to get away from there. To avoid going through the gate, which could be guarded, I decided to circle past the pit, around the back wall and from there through the fields to the road . . .

Solly believes that when Kuki had finally finished speaking, "I was certain of one thing. None of us would ever be the same again." Kuki asked Solly to go with him to see his parents that evening when they returned from work. As his parents both had jobs outside of the ghetto, they had avoided the massacre. They were afraid that the shock of seeing Kuki would be too much for them. They planned that Solly would break the news first, then Kuki would show himself. Later that night, after Kuki had been cleaned up even more, he and Solly slipped through the dark streets. Kuki hid and Solly stood and waited until he saw two shabby, old, depressed people, Mr. Kopelman and the violinist Mrs. Kopelman, Vera Shore—who had once been so elegant and worldly—walking toward the house. When Vera Shore recognized Solly in the gloom she invited him inside. "There are some books here that I am sure Kuki would want you to have," she told him. When they were inside and seated in chairs, he blurted out, "Kuki's alive!" Both jumped up. Solly warned them, "For God's sake, no one must know that he was at the fort, or we are all dead," and went to the door and gave the signal. Quickly Kuki slipped inside and Solly slipped away, weeping.

Once Kuki was back, Chaim, Solly and Kuki realized that it would be too dangerous for Kuki if people knew, so they decided not to speak about his survival. It was Chaim's idea that they describe his harrowing escape in writing, in some way, in a journal, in a diary—just so it was recorded. They made a pact that if any one of them lived, he'd see that his testimony would be published and wrote everything down exactly as they remembered. But Chaim was soon to die in that room in the ghetto in his own bed before the ghetto was liquidated. His writings were lost. Kuki Kopelman and his father would eventually be deported to Auschwitz. His mother Vera Shore would be sent to Stutthoff concentration camp. Though Kuki had been granted a reprieve from death because of the persuasive intervention of his teacher, Mr. Jablonsky, he didn't return after the war, nor did his parents. Kuki's notes and writing were lost too. Only Solly lived to keep the pact and bear witness for Chaim and "the three comrades" as well.

He remembers a moment he had with Lena after one of the first slaughters from which they'd both been spared that he'd also described in his memoir: "We waited and then cautiously opened the door. The street was deserted. We hugged and kissed . . . and said the Gomel—the blessing said by Jews who escape sudden death. At the door I asked Lena for Chaim's overdue book. She threw the book at me and screamed: 'Here, take your precious book! I bet when we're all dead you'll still be around reading your damned books!' In years to come, in the worst of times, I always remembered Lena's words. Indirectly she implied that I was insensitive but a survivor. She made me feel guilty, but strangely, she also encouraged me to go on, against all odds. Her words would prove to be prophetic."

I asked him, "Is there anything more you remember about Jablonsky?" He answered, "Although I am not a religious person, I say Kaddish for Mr. Jablonsky from time to time. I don't know why I say it for him, I hardly knew the man, but Kuki's story and Jablonsky's efforts to save Kuki left an indelible memory of him in my mind."

In his memoir, Solly lyrically describes the beauty of orange groves in Israel that burst into blossom in April around the time when Holocaust Memorial Day—Yom Hashoah—is marked. Reading his words, I can almost smell the tangy odor of orange blossoms. Although the dead are never far from Solly and every survivor I've encountered, on that day in April, those who perished are especially mourned by all of us. For Solly this includes most of his family, his neighbors and the special youthful friendship he had with Kuki and Lena that has never in his life since been replicated.

UNCANNY LUCK

Sometimes a crumb falls
From the table of joy
Sometimes a bone is flung

"LUCK"—*Langston Hughes*

After repeated efforts beginning in 1948, Nahum Kohn was finally allowed to immigrate to Canada in 1972. He'd been honored and decorated for his heroism by the Soviets for the five brutal years he spent, first as a Jewish partisan fighting with other Jews and then with Russian partisans in the Ukrainian forests of Volhynia and in and around the forests near the city of Rovno during World War II. I'd discovered his memoir *A Voice from the Forest* in the early 1980s, and it had left an indelible impression on me over the years. When I tried to find out more about Kohn, whether or not he was alive, I hit blank walls. By a fluke I located his coauthor and learned that Kohn was indeed alive, in his middle eighties, living in Montreal. I wrote to him immediately. One morning I found his reply in my mailbox: This was one of those magic moments of connection. His letter generously offered me his cooperation.

Kohn's wife is also Jewish. He has two daughters, Olga and Helena. Both daughters have studied music in Canada. He began writing his somber history with these words: "I will tell you about a world that went crazy, a world where humans became beasts, life turned worthless, and the forest became *home*. And I also will tell you about people who refused to surrender to bestiality, people who resisted the descent into darkness. Most of them are gone, but I see them still, in their tattered rags, city boys darting from tree to tree in the forest, repaying death with death. I, too, was a city boy, and although I survived, I have never really left those forests. They will be with me till my last breath."

Nahum—a muscular young watchmaker in his youth, from a large religious Jewish family—was living in Warsaw on the day the Germans attacked Poland in 1939. He was twenty years old. His courage had never been tested and he didn't know whether he had much or even any courage at all. He was quickly taught how to shoot a rifle, given one and told to go to Mokotowska Street to fight the Germans. When the German army had crushed Warsaw, Nahum went back to Sieradz—his hometown—and rejoined his twelve brothers and sisters and parents in his childhood home. He intended to stay there for the duration of the war, but when Jews were ordered to sew a yellow Star of David onto their clothes and seizures of young men for forced labor brigades had begun, Nahum's friend Mulish suggested they both hurry and cross the Bug River into Russian-held territory and escape the Germans. Nahum told Mulish that he had family responsibilities and couldn't go with him, but when his mother and father were consulted, they told him to go, and—pulling the Star of David off his shirt—he did just that.

When Nahum left home, he went from Sieradz near the

Polish–German border by train back to Warsaw, then, also by train, to Malkinia, close to the Ukrainian border. The train was full of Germans holding vicious dogs who stopped it and made everyone get off. They began searching for Jews, beating and robbing them of their valuables. Seeing this, Nahum pulled off the shoulder pads into which his sister had sewn some money and threw them away. "I figured that if it wouldn't be mine then it wouldn't be theirs either." He kept only a few zlotys, his shirts, shoes, watchmaker's tools, bread and the address of a friend of his father's. He and Mulish became separated. "Two Germans came over and gave me several good blows. I bore up well because I was in very good shape." Afterward the Germans released him and he wandered into the forest. Although he had never before been in the forest, and felt disoriented and lost at first, he was to live in various forests for most of the next five years—winter and summer.

But first, from Czyzewo he went to Bialystok, where he ran out of money and sold his hat for food. Next he went on to Kovel, then Lutsk, where a kind watchmaker named Shloime Mechlin gave him work repairing watches. From Lutsk he traveled to Tsuman, then on to the Jewish village of Trochenbrot, finding work again, this time repairing old clocks in exchange for food until—in June of 1941—the German–Russian war caught up to him, and Ukrainian nationalists who collaborated with the Germans began to attack Jewish villages. At this point Kohn had been joined by his brother Laizer and their friend Kalman Klein. Observing the worsening victimization of Jews, he commented to his brother and friend, "Why should we let such scum do whatever they want? Let's do something on our own!" Although he knew nothing about either the woods or fighting, he recruited a small group of young people, began to look for weapons and moved into the dark forest as his base of resistance. By summer of 1942, his band had eighteen Jews. And, when Jews in Trochenbrot were slaughtered by Ukrainian nationalists, "We found out which Ukrainian nationalists were in on it. We found them, took them away and killed them. That's the way the months passed, with fighting and more fighting. One of us fell, then another and another."

Nahum and his partisans didn't stay long in any part of the forest. Every day or every few days they moved twenty or thirty kilometers, staying out of reach of the Germans who hunted them constantly. They would dig holes in the ground, soften the walls with moss and sleep there. When lice infested their clothing, they'd roast them over the fire until the scorched lice fell away. When they went into a village or town to avenge Jews murdered by Ukrainian nationalists who were collaborating with the Germans, they'd exact revenge—murder for murder if possible—and dash back into the woods, leaving no trace of their whereabouts. Often during a Jewish massacre the perpetrators would rape and inflict gross brutalities on the young girls of the village. Decades later, from the safety of his home in Montreal, Kohn bitterly wrote of these bestialities: "After all these terrible things, they took thick sharpened stakes and drove them up the girls' vaginas—drove the stakes until the girls died. I'm sure that even in the tenth century, one thousand years ago, there was not such sadism. And they committed many other crimes—it's hard to explain it to you. I don't even want to remember such sadistic activities—I've spent the last thirty years trying to forget them. What they did to old people, infants, small children—ah! ah!"

After he'd been living in the forest for over a year with his group of eighteen Jewish partisans, his daredevil exploits became

well known among the Germans and their Ukrainian collaborators. Kohn had become tough, resourceful, unforgiving, fearless.
From some untapped source, brazen courage flowed. He became
notorious, known as "the watchmaker from Tsuman," and—though
a half a kilogram of salt was the reward given to anyone that murdered or captured a Jew—the reward posted for the murder
of "the watchman from Tsuman" was two kilograms of salt. And if
"the watchman from Tsuman" was brought in alive, the reward
would be five kilograms of salt. Most of his group died in one dis-
astrous skirmish, so Kohn and the two surviving men from his
group decided to join up with an antifascist Ukrainian partisan
group to continue to fight the Germans. After searching for many
months, he and his followers contacted and joined the infamous
antifascist partisans of nobleman Aleksandr Fyodorovich Felyuk
in the forest near Trochenbrot in late spring of 1942. This group
was made up of women as well as men. Kohn fought with Felyuk
until Kohn was shot and gravely wounded while pursuing a German collaborator.

While recovering from these injuries, Kohn was invited to
join the most famous and deadly Soviet partisan *atrad*, or detachment, in the Rovno area led by the intelligence expert D. M.
Medvedev. Kohn took on the alias Mietek "Misha" Kowalski and
in the beginning of 1943—because of his knowledge of watch-
making and timing—became an expert in devising detonators for
demolition, blowing up various railroad lines and trains carrying vital troops and equipment. Next he worked with Nikolay
Ivanovich Kuznetsov, who, using many aliases and often disguised
as a German officer, assassinated at least nine senior German gen-
erals including General Alfred Funk, chief judge of the Ukraine,
and other German officers. Kohn's specialty became military in-

telligence. Because he had avoided death so many times, his nick-name changed again, he became known as "Vezuchiy"—the lucky one. Once, after completing an exhausting and lengthy assign-ment near the village of Derazhno on horseback, one of his fa-tigued fellow partisans on foot begged to trade places with him temporarily. Kohn agreed, dismounted and walked on as the fel-low galloped off on his horse. Soon he heard an explosion up ahead. His horse had stepped on a buried mine, was blown to bits. Although the rider briefly lived, his wounds were mortal and he too died.

After a small group of partisans, Nahum at the head, had blown up a train, they were attacked by Germans and police, and many of his group were killed or wounded. The survivors trav-eled through the forest in the night and only stopped for a rest at dawn. His comrades gathered around him and began to laugh. One said, "You're a *vesuchiy*. I heard about your past adventures. No bullet can down you!" Another added, "You certainly deserve that name!" Then Nahum noticed that the bulky jacket he'd been wearing unbuttoned had been pierced by bullet holes in several places. He took off the jacket, held it up and realized that he could see through the holes though not one bullet had even grazed his flesh.

His determination to resist the Nazis and exact revenge re-mained undaunted. By summer of 1943, his *atrad* was based in the thick forests near Tsuman. One day a weak moaning sound was heard in the forest. The partisans discovered a small, skeletal, hairless being with eyeballs popping who had survived the slaugh-ter of the entire Jewish population in a small village. The *atrad* res-cued the being near starvation, fed and cared for him. His name was Pinya, he was a minute Jewish boy whom they adopted and protected and eventually sent to a special school in Moscow. After the Germans had retreated from Russia and the Ukraine, Nahum and the twenty-five surviving members of his *atrad* were ordered to Kiev. The distance to Kiev was about four hundred miles. It took them five days and nights to cross the ravaged countryside. When they arrived in Kiev, they were given a heroes' welcome. "A crowd of civilians quickly grew around us. They had never seen partisans before. We carried our weapons proudly, and we were a crusty lot—we must have given those civilians quite an eyeful!"

As honored heroes, they were sent to a farm near Kiev, given special cabins and a cook. The cook was told to prepare whatever would please them. There, while he waited for the war to end in Europe, Nahum returned to work repairing clocks and watches in a government shop. He quickly sent a barrage of letters to the police, to neighbors, to city hall in Sieradz, begging for news of his

Nahum Kohn (*left*) and fellow partisans in the Tsuman forest, the Ukraine.

family. He waited. When news arrived that his entire family had been killed, he began to drink heavily. At one point his brother-in-arms from the years in the forests, the partisan Mikkail Kutavoy, visited him. Kutavoy watched Kohn swallow drink after drink. Kutavoy was so distressed by such drinking that he slapped Nahum across the face, said, "I came to Kiev to find my Nahum. And who do I see? A goddamn drink, that's who!" Kohn spread out the letters from Sieradz, told Mikkail, "When I received those letters, I asked myself: Why did I remain alive? Why did I survive? And I started to drink. When I drank, I used to feel that they were all alive, with me, near me. Many times I used to return to my room and start to cry. I saw one fellow-worker going with a brother, another with a sister, but I was like a lost sheep. The flock had gone in one direction and I had gone off in another direction, and I was lost. I used to cry like a lost sheep that bleats in its panic and solitude, all alone. Look at my hair, Mikkail." During the early years in the forest Nahum's hair had been jet black. Mikkail looked and realized that although the war was over only a short time, and Kohn was not even twenty-five years old yet, his hair was completely white.

Stunned by Mikkail's words and by his concern, Kohn smashed the remaining store of whiskey bottles. From that day into old age, he's barely touched a drop of alcohol. In 1948, he left Kiev and relocated in Rovno, where he discovered that one of his first cousins had actually survived and was living in Minsk. He journeyed to Minsk to see her. When the cousins set eyes on each other, the emotions were volatile. "We were sobbing and our bodies were shaking. As for myself, I couldn't say one word—I was struck speechless. The next day we regained our composure and we spoke nonstop for hours on end." Among other news, she told him that she'd heard through her sister living in Belgium that his brother Fyvel, also known as Felix, was alive. Nahum remembers that the instant she'd spoken those words, goose pimples broke out all over him and he began to shiver. It took weeks for him to follow the trail of clues as to his brother's whereabouts and discovered that his brother was living in Israel. But it wasn't until 1964, on his first trip back to Poland, that they were able to meet each other again. "There was a knock at the front door, so I opened it. A man, one head taller than I was, was standing there with two valises at his feet. He said, 'Nahum?' I blurted out, 'Felix?' He said, 'Yes.' We embraced but we were both speechless. We sat for twenty minutes, paralyzed and speechless."

The brothers sat together for two hours in silence. Then Felix suggested a walk. So they walked, not exchanging one word. They came to a park, rested on a bench. A half hour passed. The silence continued. Finally, Nahum managed to say a few words. "All of a sudden, tears poured out of Felix's eyes like a fountain. This lasted for half an hour, but I had no sooner calmed him down when I myself started to cry, uncontrollably, spasmodically. Now it was his turn to calm me down, and that took another forty minutes or so. We walked over to a fountain and washed our faces to hide the traces of the tears. We sat for ten more minutes in the park, and said a few words to each other. Out of twelve brothers and sisters, only the two of us were left, and the rest—gone with the wind."

In the final winter of the war, Kati Kadelburger was twelve years old. From an affluent Hungarian Jewish family, Kati, her mother, brother and grandmother had avoided deportation to

Portrait of Kati Kadelburger, by M. Kôvesy Albi, painted in Budapest in 1944.

Auschwitz because they'd received *Schutzpässe*—protective pass-ports—from the Swedish diplomat Raoul Wallenberg. When the bombings of Budapest began, they converted the cellar of her grandmother's large three-story Budapest house at Laudon Utca No. 1 into an air raid shelter. They offered shelter to some of their household help, to neighbors—Christian and Jewish. Except for Kati's brother Gustav, who had become a messenger for Wallenberg, most of those they sheltered were women. Most men had already been deported as forced labor or been sent to concentration camps—as had her father, who'd died quite early in the war.

It was during a visit to Budapest to participate in a Holocaust event sponsored by the Hungarian government that I met Kati Kadelburger, the young girl who'd lived through the terrible bombardment of Budapest in the cellar of her grandmother's house. When we met, she had lived in Stockholm for many years and had married a Swede. We'd both come to Budapest to participate in the same event, a photo exhibition called Visas for Life. It would be hung in the National Library and would contain photos of diplomats—Raoul Wallenberg, Carl Lutz, Per Anger, Chiune Sugihara and others—who'd risked their lives to help save endangered Jewish people. The career diplomat Per Anger was the only one of these men still living. Although he was in his eighties, he and his wife would be coming to Budapest and would be honored at a ceremony. Kati Kadelburger, now called Kate Wacz, was small, well-dressed and carefully coiffed. She was also energetic, gregarious, and very quickly offered her services to me as a guide. After she'd taken me to see the newly renovated Nagy Zsinagoga—the Byzantine-Moorish Great Synagogue—on Sohany Street on whose grand organ Liszt and Saint-Saëns had played and in whose courtyard a metal weeping willow tree honored the victims of the Holocaust—Kate and I sat across from each other at a good Hungarian restaurant. It was warm, cozy. She advised me on ordering from an untranslated menu.

When our food had been eaten, we lingered over fruit tortes and strong coffee. She explained that her family had owned a Swedish steel company before the war, and that after the war her mother had gone to Sweden to try to reclaim the company. "After the war my mother and brother had gone to live in Sweden to pick up the pieces and run the company again. I had started at my high school in Hungary by then. My mother took me to Sweden for a visit when I was sixteen. She wanted me to stay but I preferred to go back and go to school in Hungary and did. I didn't understand or care about politics. So she took me back to Budapest, left me, returning to Sweden. Mother married a Swede and became a Swedish citizen in 1948. Then—because of the Soviet occupation—I couldn't get out of Hungary and Mother couldn't get back in. Mother started to negotiate through the Swedish foreign office for my exit visa. In 1951, I finally came to Sweden."

I saw Kati again in New York. She was staying at a Midtown hotel and we met in the hotel coffee shop. Although she was in her late sixties, she looked much younger. She was a career woman in Sweden and looked it, was chic, wore expensive clothes and shoes. I began where we'd left off our conversation in Budapest: "You told me that after the war your mother remarried and stayed in Sweden?" "Yes, that's true." Then I inquired about her separation from her mother. "You said that you didn't see your mother for three years?" A welter of strong feeling suddenly overwhelmed her and she began to cry. I quickly switched off my tape recorder. We sat silently for several minutes until Kate wiped her eyes and indicated that she wanted to begin taping once again. Then she took us back to Budapest during wartime.

In that winter of 1945, the Red Army had been shelling Budapest for two months, sending wave after wave of bombers roaring through the sky, destroying much of the sprawling, historical city. Outside the damaged hulk of their house, Hungarian Nazi gangs—Nyilas, or Arrow Cross, in their green shirts and black

ties—roamed the streets and buildings in search of Jews. On finding a Jew, the Nyilas would round him up and force him to the
very edge of the Danube. Then they would shoot at close range so
that the body would fall into the river. The blood of the murdered
people flowed until their bodies froze onto the ice chunks. Famine
was spreading through the city, as was an epidemic of typhus. Below ground, in their cellar, Kati lay in her makeshift bed covered
by her grandma's old fur coat. She and the others in the shelter
huddled together. They rarely slept, since the explosions could
be heard and vibrations felt day and night. Candlelight was their
only source of light. "We were lucky," Kati commented.

At one point, despite their Swedish protection, her family was
made to go out into the street where they were assembled with
other Jews, marched through the streets and crammed into a
small room somewhere by Nyilas. "On January seventh we were
taken in the night. The Arrow Cross shouted at us. We thought
we'd be brought to the Danube and killed. The Arrow Cross
squeezed two hundred eighty people into one room. It was horrible. My cousin was on my uncle's shoulders. I was on my brother's
shoulders. We didn't know if we'd die the next minute or the next
day. We stayed there all night. The next day we were marched out
in single file. They made us empty our pockets. I had to take off
my boots. I didn't think twice about the boots but regretted that
the nuts I had in my pocket—cashew nuts—were taken away." For
a second I was taken aback by her statement about the cashew
nuts. Was she being ironical? Then I remembered that she'd been
twelve at the time, and to a twelve-year-old, the loss of a handful
of cashew nuts can mean more than the loss of a pair of boots in
winter. She continued: "Then we were lined up and marched to

the Danube. But, I have no idea why, they didn't shoot us like they'd shot so many others. We were released and allowed to go home."

By February, the food supply in the cellar was dwindling. When the Germans surrendered to the Red Army on February 14, 1945, some fifty thousand unburied civilian bodies lay under rubble and snow. The Russian soldiers were jubilant as they entered the once regal twin cities of Buda and Pest along the frozen Danube. They were cold and hungry, filthy and exhausted. They quickly discovered that there was very little to loot as they went from house to house amidst the ruins. When a small patrol of soldiers waving Sten guns pushed through the shrapnel-riddled door of the Kadelburger house, they climbed down the steps into the cellar to pillage. They wanted three things—alcohol, wristwatches and women.

On reaching the cellar the occupants cowered—the soldiers found no wristwatches. One soldier noticed Grandma's bottle of French eau de cologne and swilled it down in one swallow. Another announced that he would be taking a woman to have sex with and asked for a volunteer. No one volunteered. He eyed the women. His gaze fell on Kati. He exclaimed, "I'll take *her*." When relating this part of her story, Kati modestly lowered her voice. She continued speaking almost in a whisper, "The soldier that stared at me grabbed my long braids and began to pull me toward the stairway by my hair. Grandma pleaded, 'Please. She's a little girl. A baby. She's a virgin. Leave her alone! I beg of you.' A neighbor who'd been in the shelter for the entire time and had a daughter too pointed to Grandma's old fur coat. This woman turned her gaze on Grandma, and announced, 'If you let me have this coat, I'll go instead of her.' Grandma handed her the coat. The woman put it on. She went up the stairway with the soldiers."

I turned off my tape recorder. We ordered dessert. I was struck by the fact that what could be considered dumb luck had saved a twelve-year-old girl from—at the very least—rape. And that what could be considered a random stroke of luck had saved that same girl from being murdered on the banks of the Danube on a winter night. Our waitress, a well-turned-out young redhead, about nineteen years old, delivered our cheesecake. I wondered to myself what—if anything—virginity meant to this young woman? I wondered what—if anything—this American woman's mother or grandmother would have given to save hers? I wondered how— if at all—this modern young girl or even I might survive being taken to the banks of a river by a gang of murderers and threatened with death?

I'd put away my tape recorder, and Kati and I spoke of other things—her flight back to Stockholm, a book the Swedish government had prepared to teach children about the Holocaust titled *Tell Ye Your Children . . .* As we prepared to leave, our conversation went back to the cellar and the coat. I asked, "What kind of coat was it?" "Persian lamb," she replied, "black Persian lamb. When I think of that coat today, it was nothing special. But at that time, it was precious."

On May 26, 1943, Jules Schelvis—whom I would come to know very well in his old age—was a handsome young printer from Amsterdam. He and his family were awakened from sleep by the loud, hollow sound of harsh voices broadcasting from loudspeakers. He was living with his new wife, Chel, and her Polish parents, David and Gretha Borzykowski, on Nieuwe Kerkstraat in the heart of the Jewish Quarter, which had been marked by the Germans with yellow signs on the corners of the streets since their attack and occupation of Holland in 1940. Jules got out of bed and looked out of the window. The streets were deserted. The voice blared, from a loudspeaker on top of a car, that all Jews were to prepare for departure, that no one was allowed to go out into the street, that all the bridges in the quarter had been pulled up.

From the window Jules saw in the moonlight that it was true: The Magerebrug, the bridge at the end of the street, had been pulled up. Escape was impossible. His parents, who worked in the diamond trade, and sister Milly lived in another quarter, on Henriette Ronnerstraat. He had no way of contacting them at that moment. Jules, Chel and the Borzykowskis gathered their dearest books, photographs and other things of value and hid them behind a wall. Then they packed their rucksacks and breadsacks and waited. He spoke about this frantic interval to me in a quiet voice in his living room in Tricht, Holland, a small village a few miles outside of Amsterdam. We were drinking strong Dutch coffee and eating ginger cookies, and almost sixty years had passed since the war: "At the time we still thought that the Krauts—barbarians though they were—had some remnant of civilization. We assumed that we would be made to work in camps under police surveillance, that we, the men, would have to work very hard and that the women would probably have to work in the ammunitions factories or would have to clear rubble in the bombarded towns in the east. Maybe we would not get enough food, but we would probably hold out. Yes, that was what we thought then." Jules explained to me that he imagined that the nights "in the east" in captivity would be long, so he decided to strap his guitar onto his back. He thought that playing music would help to pass the long nights.

Inside his rucksack was clothing, a water bottle. A pair of shoes was in the side compartments, and a rolled-up woolen blanket was on top under the flap. The sack also contained extra food. Straddling the rucksack was the guitar. Through the window Jules and the others saw the Grüne Polizei coming toward their building. Then they heard the doorbell ring. He pulled the handle that opened the outside door and let them into the building. All were taken downstairs and marched to the corner of Weesperstraat, where they were told to wait in front of Moos van Kleef's fish shop for more Jews to be brought. When the group was large enough, they were taken to the Jonas Daniël Meyer Plein and registered in the Great Synagogue. Next they were put on trams to the Muiderpoort railway station, then transported by train to the Dutch transit camp called Westerbork. On June 1, 1943, he and his wife and in-laws were packed into trains and sent to a Polish hamlet called Sobibor. Here Jules was separated from his wife and in-laws. Out of thirty-four thousand Dutch Jews who left Westerbork between March and July 1943 with Sobibor as their destination, Jules was one of three men who survived. Today there's a nature reserve and scenic picnic stop beside what was the Sobibor stop on the rail line. Today, only a watchtower and the commandant's house remain as monuments to the place in which hundreds of thousands met death, where an SS officer enjoyed putting a tin bucket onto a Jew's head like a top hat and practicing his shooting. Where once stood the camp and where a gas chamber once sent flames licking the sky stands a monument of a woman

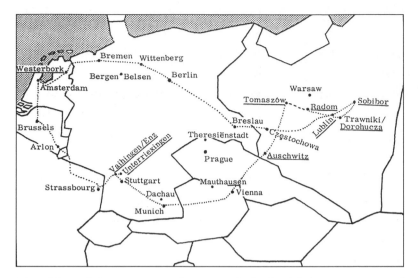

Map of Central Europe. Names of camps in which Jules Schelvis was imprisoned are underlined.

holding a child in her arms. Another monument is a tall block of rectangular stone.

Besides his statistic-defying survival of Sobibor, Jules further defied his statistical chances at Auschwitz, Dorohucza, Lublin, Radom, Tomaszow, Unterriexingen and Vaihingen. "How?" I asked him, incredulous after hearing the daunting names of all the places in which he'd been imprisoned. Jules joined the thumb and forefinger of his left hand to the thumb and forefinger of his right like links in a chain and pulled, straining. "The chain held." Demonstrating again, he explained, "Each time . . . again and again . . . the chain simply held."

On April 5, 1945, in Vaihingen, Jules remembers: "Our guards left the camp. They came down from the watchtowers and walked away quietly as if they had never had anything at all to do with us.

Their guns hung loosely on their shoulders. I watched them leave till they were out of sight." Not knowing what to do, Jules and the few other living prisoners simply waited. "That evening I went to bed late and slept restlessly. I thought it was because of all the emotions of the nerve-racking day. But the next morning, I ran a very high fever and was not able to get up. The diagnosis was typhoid. I was near despair. For two years I had lived through misery again and again, hoping that a miracle would happen, that I would survive this damned war and that I would return to my beloved Amsterdam where I hoped I would find someone left, maybe, of my family or friends. And now, at the end of the race, with one foot over the finish line, now I caught typhoid. A dangerous illness in a camp."

Delirious, with a high fever, he passed three days and nights. On April 8, a French officer entered the barrack. The officer spoke words no one understood; he gave the prisoners cigarettes, chocolates and shook hands with those who were able to lift their hands. "Some of us, who could still weep, let their tears run freely. For me, at this important moment, there was no joy. I had imagined the splendor of liberation so very differently. To die, after liberation had come . . . I wanted to go out too and plunder the village, just like some others, to take back the radios and bicycles that the Krauts had stolen from us, long ago, at home." The French set up a field hospital to treat the sick. "Skilled French nurses helped me shower and took care of me in a most touching way. Dressed in a pair of neat pajamas, I was then carried into one of the waiting ambulances, which brought me to the Vaihingen–Enz hospital." Gravely ill, he lay in hospital from April 15 until June 20.

When at last his physical health had rallied and he was well enough to travel, he set out for home. His route took him through Strasbourg, Nancy, Arlon at the Belgium–Luxembourg border, then on through Brussels to the Dutch border at Oudenbosch. "At the railway station of Oudenbosch, I got out of the carriage, to demonstratively stand on Dutch soil again. The lump in my throat was too big for me to utter a sound."

In Amsterdam he walked and walked, simply breathing in the air of liberated Amsterdam. From the Koningsplein he walked toward the Herengracht. "I walked down the Herengracht, to the Amstel River, where I got to the Nieuwe Prinsengracht by the Magerebrug. No one seemed to notice me; it was as if I belonged to the many Amsterdammers who had gotten through the famine winter. I wanted to cry out to everyone I met that I was one of the very few exceptions who had come back from the extermination camps of Sobibor and Auschwitz. That I had been in Dorohucza, Lublin and Unterriexingen. That I had returned from Hell. But this was the worst dream of the past two years. Returning to the reality of the moment, I went, weeping openly. Everything had truly happened, and there was no one to comfort me. All those I had loved were no more. Murdered!"

SUPERNATURAL FACTORS

Sir: If a miracle is an event without a physical cause then miracles occur in abundance. Whenever an electron passes through a diffraction grating (which displays the nature of waves) it can then be detected as moving along one of several exit channels provided for it by the grating.

Despite intense efforts, no physical cause has ever been found for the choice of channel, or for similar choices made in many other physical processes. Modern physicists have concluded that no such cause exists. Or, in other words, that the cause is nonphysical. It is usually attributed to "chance," but that of course is simply an evasion.

Yours truly,
Alan Cottrell
Cambridge, England

Sir: With respect to both those seeking the canonization of the late Mother Teresa and those discussing the claimed miraculous powers of a silver medallion touched by her body after her death . . . life itself is the miracle. Try making something as "simple" as a mosquito if you don't believe me . . .

Yours faithfully,
Richard N. Strange
London, England

Sir: The great difficulty with miracles is not whether God performs such things, but whether any Being capable of being regarded as God could wish to behave in such an arbitrary and callous way. If miracles actually happen, then God stands condemned.

Yours faithfully,
Michael Tatham
Buckinghamshire, England

LETTERS TO THE EDITOR, THE TIMES (LONDON),

SEPTEMBER 10, 2001

Joseph Bau's mother, Tzilah Bau, originally from Krakow, Poland, died—"was murdered" is how Joseph refers to her death—in Bergen-Belsen concentration camp. His father, Abraham, was murdered in Plaszow concentration camp, and his brother Iziu (Ignacy) was murdered in the Krakow ghetto. Joseph's own survival, the mysterious coincidences that kept him and his brother Marcel alive in Plaszow, Joseph's clandestine marriage while a prisoner at Plaszow and the reunion with his wife after their separation defied all the odds. Or, as Bau himself explains so much good fortune, "defied the laws of nature." The word he uses liberally to describe these events is one that's usually used as a sign of divine intervention in human affairs, the repeated word he chooses—"miracle."

In 1971, Joseph Bau and his wife, Rebecca, reluctantly returned to Europe—to Austria—from Israel, where they'd lived since war's end. In Israel, Bau had become a renowned artist, an animator, and also an author. After I contacted him, we conducted our interview by e-mail. He was eager to discuss his life. But one day his children e-mailed me to say their father was ill and in the hospital. Fortunately, whatever else I needed to know could be found in his book of writing and sardonic drawings, *Dear God, Have You Ever Gone Hungry?*

Because Joseph had been a witness to many brutal murders committed by an SS officer named Franz Gruen—including the murder of his own father—at Plaszow, he was invited to act as a witness by the Austrian government at Gruen's trial. Gruen was eventually sentenced to nine years in prison, and, as Joseph later explained, the effect of seeing Gruen, of returning to a German-speaking country in Europe, of recounting the bitter facts of his father's murder, caused his eyesight to blur, his mind to hallucinate scenes from the gruesome past, his blood pressure to shoot up so high he ended up in a Viennese hospital for an entire month. Except for several visits by his old friend and benefactor Oskar Schindler, it seemed to Bau from the Austrian hospital bed that he had fallen into—in his words—"a pit full of scorpions and snakes." He didn't feel safe until he returned to Israel.

But even in Israel, regardless of the many decades that passed after the war, images of persecution, privation, brutality remained vividly alive in his memory. For instance, one Saturday evening, as Joseph and his wife and children sat at the dinner table after a fine meal, these images came to haunt him. The table had been set with a good tablecloth. The room was lit by candles. Rebecca had just cut and distributed slices of cake, topped with icing and powdered sugar, that she herself had baked. Music was playing on the radio in the background. Joseph remembers watching his wife. He remembers the mouthful of delicious cake sticking in his throat. "Suddenly, I saw her in the striped dress, with a white kerchief on her shaven head, looking at me with sad, hollow eyes. The light dimmed, and emaciated shadows dressed in prison uniforms surrounded me again. The chill wind brought the sound of shooting in the distance, and my nostrils breathed in the smell of burning flesh." Bau spit out the cake, which to him tasted like stone. Although part of him returned to reality—he could hear the music on the radio, see his children eating the delicious cake—another part of him remained, and will forever remain, in the concentration camp that dwells inside.

First miracle: In the second winter of the war, in Krakow, the streets were frozen with sleet, and a nasty Siberian wind blew snow and ice against buildings, trees and lamp poles. At the time, Joseph and his brother Marcel had badly forged papers; they'd been denied the yellow identity cards, *Kennkarten,* that the police had issued certain Jews but not others. Thus they were constantly in danger of deportation and so slept in the home of a Christian, a chimney sweep, at night. They could not go to their own bed in daytime, and were forced to stay outdoors. This was excruciating because the weather was terribly cold. Their younger brother, Iziu, age ten, was sometimes able to bring them a pot of their mother's hot soup. But sometimes he couldn't make it, and Joseph and Marcel had nothing to eat.

One very dark night, Joseph and Marcel were making their way back to their rented couch in time for the curfew. As they approached the bridge, someone warned them that an SS officer was blocking that bridge and shooting at any Jew who tried to cross. Joseph and Marcel ran in another direction into a strange neighborhood. Just then, all the lights in the town went out due to a power outage. Disoriented, they wandered through dark streets. They kept walking and realized they had drifted away from the town and were walking in mud through a field. They could hear the sound of a flowing river; it was so dark that they could see nothing before them but looming shapes. They groped their way in another direction and found themselves in an unfamiliar neighborhood, had no idea where they were. They were freezing now, lost and exhausted. Seeing candles burning in the window of a house, they remembered that it was the first night of Hanukkah. Something made them walk toward this flickering candlelight. When they got almost to the door of the house, they realized that they'd walked right to the door of the chimney sweep. They entered and the chimney sweep explained the power failure and told them he'd lit candles in the front room for them.

In Joseph's words: "To this day, I'm unable to explain how we managed to reach that house in the gloomy night, how we crossed the river and the air base without being aware of it." Even when he examined the town after the war, he could not unravel the route taken. He concludes: "The mystery can only be explained as our private Hanukkah miracle."

Eventually Marcel and Joseph went to the Krakow ghetto with their family, but then were sent to the Plaszow work camp. At Plaszow, night and day, the white smoke of those who had died that day rose from the crematorium and the stink of burning human remains filled the air. Joseph describes that grim sight: "The departed in the form of white smoke, rose easily upward, waved their hands in parting and viewed with pity all those who remained behind. Then they danced gaily in celebration of their new freedom, before disintegrating in the air."

Because of his drawing skills, Joseph was given the job of drawing plans and signs or anything else that needed to be designed or painted. His mother worked outside the camp every day. Marcel was sent to the Jewish cemetery, where he was ordered to smash headstones with a sledgehammer. The pieces of this sacred stone would be used for paving roads. One morning Marcel confided to Joseph that he'd found a priceless gold cup in the cemetery and had hidden it. "It's worth a fortune!" Marcel told him. Joseph looked at the tarnished but obviously pure gold cup and was alarmed. He urged his brother to get rid of it. And quickly.

That night, he and Marcel were planning to visit their mother, hoping, since she worked on the outside of the camp and could often scrounge up extra food to bring home for her sons, that she'd bring some with her. After Joseph had begun his day's work of painting, writing slogans, he heard in the distance the sound of sledgehammers. Among them would be his brother Marcel. Late that afternoon Joseph heard that a hanging was going to occur that night. When he inquired as to who would be hanged and why, he was told that someone had been caught with stolen gold. The rumor was that the person who would be hanged had a short name that began with the letter B. Joseph didn't need to hear any more—he wept, knowing that they'd caught Marcel.

As he walked toward his mother's barrack, he could almost hear the sound of Kaddish in the sound of the blowing wind. He found his mother back in the barrack. She told him she had a great surprise. To go with their ration of bread and margarine, she had a boiled egg and a slice of onion to share among the three of them. Ashamed, unable to tell his mother the truth, he pretended to have a headache and left the barrack. Joseph was walking aimlessly when Marcel appeared from nowhere and announced that he'd sold the gold on the black market. "I watched him with wonder and joy," was how Joseph described the emotion he felt. Eventually, he discovered that the hanged boy was named Beim. The Germans had found a gold watch in Beim's pocket.

Second miracle: Joseph first met the woman who would be-

Drawing by Joseph Bau.

come his wife—who wore the usual striped uniform of a prisoner, her shaved head covered by a white kerchief—while he stood outside an office in Plaszow. He was drafting a map. He of course had no way of knowing then that they'd live together for fifty-three years until her death in 1997, or that he would outlive her. Although men and women had been executed if they were caught making love or even holding hands, Joseph found a few wildflowers and hid them in his cap. He went to look for the woman he'd seen whose name he had been told was Rebecca. He met her in the soup line and began a courtship. To locate each other, they whistled a short tune that became their trademark. Joseph acquired a white kerchief and—as did women prisoners—wore it over his shaved head in order to pass as a woman. Joseph and Rebecca kissed for the first time behind the latrine as the moon shone down. They decided that they wanted to marry each other. But how could this be done in such a place?

It took four black-market loaves of bread made with brown flour and sawdust to buy one spoon that was made of good silver. And it took four more loaves of this same bread as a bribe to a prisoner who had been a jeweler to make two wedding rings out of the acquired silver spoon. On a chosen evening, Joseph and Rebecca met beside his mother's three-tier bunk. Despite the fact that they couldn't find a rabbi to do the service, they crafted a makeshift wedding. "Harei at..." concluded Joseph. Joseph's mother gave her blessings. In their eyes, and—they hoped—in the eyes of God, they were man and wife. They decided to share her bed that night, which was a dangerous act indeed but worth the risk.

But just as they'd climbed up to the top bunk and were becoming acquainted with each other at close, intimate quarters, news that the Germans were going to conduct a search of the women's barracks was broadcast over the loudspeaker. The several women who slept next to Rebecca spread Joseph with filthy rags and laid their heads on him as though he were a pillow. He wasn't detected during the search, but almost immediately after it was concluded, the siren signaled an unscheduled count of male prisoners. This meant that all men were to go quickly to the assembly grounds to be counted. Absence or lateness meant death. Adjusting the white kerchief back onto his head, Joseph jumped down from the three-tier bunk and ran toward the men's camp as the floodlights swept pools of light back and forth across the grounds. He reached the fence that divided the men's and women's sections only to discover that the usually open gate of the high fence had been closed and electrified. If he touched it, he would die from bolts of electricity. If he didn't quickly reach the assembly point, he'd die in some other way. He decided to try to make an impossible leap. Still amazed more than fifty years later, Joseph says of his leap, "I rose, unwittingly, so high that only my fingers and toes grazed the strands with the lethal current. To this day, I cannot understand how I managed to cheat that mad trap, the dragon that spit fire and swallowed even the bravest heroes. By rights, I should have found my death then and there!"

But soon Joseph was marked for death again. Plans were afoot to transfer Joseph and many other prisoners from Plaszow, which was in the process of being shut down, to an even more lethal concentration camp named Gross-Rosen. At the time, Rebecca had become manicurist for an infamously sadistic Nazi, Amon Goeth, who kept a loaded gun beside the manicure table. If Rebecca's manicure scissors slipped and cut him, she was told, he would shoot her. During her visits to Goeth's house, she became acquainted with his secretary, who was a Jewish prisoner named Mietek Pemper who had come to Plaszow with his mother. Because Rebecca had successfully intervened when Pemper's mother was about to be shot—and saved her life—to return the favor, Pemper offered to add Rebecca's name to the list he was presently assembling of Jews who would be sent to work in a factory in Czechoslovakia. The owner of the factory was named Oskar Schindler. When the moment came to add her name to the list that would one day become known as "Schindler's List," Rebecca wrote down Joseph Bau's name and not her own. So when the bitter day of parting came, Joseph was transferred and went to work in Schindler's factory in Czechoslovakia, where he was protected and fed by Oskar and Emilie Schindler at Brinnlitz. Rebecca remained at Plaszow but was soon sent to Auschwitz, where she survived three selections to the gas chamber. She was later taken to Lichtwerden in Czechoslovakia. Her substitution of his name for hers was never mentioned after the war to anyone, not even to her husband. Forty years later, Joseph finally learned the truth when Rebecca revealed it in the making of the film *Schindler's List*.

Neither could have imagined ever seeing the other again, on the terrible day of their separation. Joseph had left his "dear and sacred love" a poem that includes the lines

> *Though our life together was so short,*
> *I must leave now.*
> *Sad and forlorn, I am going*
> *To a fate ordained by these desperate times,*
> *By a road unmarked by any signs,*
> *To a mocking destiny*
> *All set to welcome me.*

Despite the protection he was given by the Schindlers, Joseph weighed sixty-six pounds when the Russian army liberated Brinnlitz. Almost immediately, along with a small group of survivors, he began the arduous task of trying to get back home. He hoped that if his wife or any of his family had survived, they'd go home too. He jumped freight trains, crossed borders on foot, he somehow made his way to the street in Krakow to the house where his family had lived. Though he found their apartment occupied by a knife-wielding man, he was elated to be home. He found lodging elsewhere and began visiting the Jewish Committee office, which daily posted lists of living and dead. Here Joseph discovered that his mother, once a respected couturier who had owned her own boutique specializing in hats, had died in Germany in Bergen-Belsen. He learned that though she had managed to hang on to life, she had died shortly after the camp was liberated by the British. Eventually, he discovered that Marcel had survived in Germany and so had Rebecca. Although Rebecca had finished the war in Lichtwerden, she had been in an accident in the small city of Freudenthal. She and several women were in a wagon being taken somewhere when the wagon overturned. All the women were injured and had been put in a hospital there. But how to get to Freudenthal? First he had to find a way to be issued a travel permit.

Miracle upon miracle: Joseph wrangled a travel permit. Desperate to get to Rebecca, he began jumping freight trains again. At the juncture of Morawska Ostrowa, he was instructed by the trainmaster to get on the train to Szwinow and jump off while the train was still moving, and there transfer to Freudenthal. Joseph found his crowded train and squeezed on board. Wanting to be ready to jump, he sat in an open door frame, legs hanging down dangerously outside the moving train. He tried to stay awake but sleep overcame him, and when he woke he discovered he'd missed the spot where he was to leap. He got off the train at the next station to find out that not only had he missed his disembarkation spot, but he'd also missed the connecting train. Amidst great confusion at the train station, Joseph found a train going back in the direction he'd come. He climbed onto the flat roof of the train, and it began its journey. Shortly, however, dark clouds gathered and a storm broke open, pouring hail and heavy rain down on the roof of the train. Soaked, bones aching, he managed to stay alert, and got off the train at the transfer point, Szwinow. In a sorry state, shivering, hungry, Joseph waited for a connecting train and climbed aboard. It happened to be a passenger train. He found a normal seat and fell asleep.

Abruptly his deep sleep was interrupted when the train stopped and all the passengers were ordered off the train. Again confusion reigned. His clothing—the prisoner's striped shirt and trousers from the camp that he still wore—was still wet. He made inquiries and learned, to his amazement, that the reason for the abrupt interruption of his journey was that there had been a recent accident with a train. It seemed that a train packed with passengers had been crossing the river on a bridge when the bridge—damaged in the war—gave way. The train had plunged into the river here in Opava where they were. People were crushed in the fall; others had drowned in the river. Further questioning revealed to Joseph that the train that had been in the accident was none other than the train he'd been trying desperately to catch. Had he not fallen asleep, had he made his connection, he would have been on that train and would most likely have died in the river.

Joseph marveled at this most recent reprieve from death as he waited beside the river through the night, watching as the clouds indifferently scuttled across the face of the moon. Out of the blue, an enraged woman singled him out, accused him—despite his vocal denials and the striped prisoner shirt he still wore—of being a German, a Nazi, a criminal. The police were called in and he was

Notes of a tune whistled by Rebecca and Joseph Bau.

taken to the police station. The situation calmed when Joseph showed his papers to the police. One policeman felt badly when he realized that Joseph was a Jewish survivor. He asked if he could help in any way. Joseph explained about his wife's injury on the overturned wagon, about his journey in search of his wife, about the trains, the bridge. "You know," said the policeman, "here in Opava we had a similar accident with a wagon. In fact, there are still several girls in the hospital."

It seemed an odd coincidence. Although Joseph believed that Rebecca was in Freudenthal, he went to the hospital in Opava with the policeman anyway. All the while, he kept protesting that his wife was in Freudenthal, not Opava. Nonetheless, in the corridor of the hospital he whistled the special notes known only to Rebecca and himself. In his own words: "I entered the hospital with the policeman and whistled the tune we'd used to locate each other at the Plaszow camp. No, I cannot find the words to describe that wonderful reunion which defied all the laws of nature. I'll leave it to you . . . to imagine what happened on that fateful evening of June 7, 1945."

When war swept Europe, the consul general of Bordeaux from neutral Portugal was a stout man of aristocratic origin named Dr. Aristides de Sousa Mendes do Amaral e Abranches. He was a devout Roman Catholic from birth to death. He and his wife, Angelina (his first cousin), had fourteen children in the course of twenty years. The girls were: Clotilde, who played the piano, studied law at university, married and had eleven children of her own; Isabel, who also married young, was cheerful, happy; Joana, spoiled and moody; and Teresinha, who refused to play the piano and couldn't stand her studies. The boys were: Aristides Jr., who liked to play the piano; Manuel, a fine student; José, a nearsighted boy who also played the piano; Geraldo, remembered for his gift of gab; Pedro Nuno, the family artist; Carlos, another pianist, who was quiet and brooding; Sebastião, the only blonde in the family; Luís Filipe, who was very smart; and João Paulo—the sensitive, quiet last surviving child. João Paulo, whom I would come to know in Los Angeles, was born in 1932, when his father was stationed in Belgium. João Paulo became the family mascot. At night, before bed and with great formality, one by one, the children would kiss their father's hand and bid him good night.

Because the family was so large, Aristides had a special bus designed in Antwerp that would accommodate all of them. It was a cream-colored minibus nicknamed "Expresso dos Montes Herminios," called by the younger children the *camionette*. Sousa Mendes had had various diplomatic postings before Bordeaux. In Demerara, British Guiana, he was posted as a second-class consul. He was later sent to Zanzibar. After that, they were sent to Curitiba and Pôrto Alegre in the southern part of Brazil. Next, he was transferred to San Francisco, then back to Pôrto Alegre. After a sojourn in Lisbon, he was assigned to Vigo, Spain, then transferred in 1929 to Antwerp, where his title was consul general. Three years later, he was moved to Louvain, also in Belgium, where João Paulo—who uses the name John Paul Abranches—was born. A little sister, Raquel, was born in 1933, but she lived only briefly; she died around the same time as her older brother Manuel. After the death of these two children, a grieving Mendes, wanting to travel farther afield than Europe, petitioned for posts in Japan and China, but was unsuccessful.

Instead, in September 1938, he was posted to Bordeaux, France, where he moved his family and various relatives into a fourteen-room house at 14 Quai Louis XVIII on an embankment with views of the Garonne River and the port of Bordeaux. He allotted several of the rooms of the house for the Portuguese consulate. In our several conversations, John Paul gave the impression that he remembers his childhood with pleasure. He learned to speak Flemish as well as French. Of course, the entire family spoke Portuguese at home. He speaks emotionally about his family, especially his father and mother, and so softly that it was necessary for me to lean in in order to hear. In several phone calls, his voice made him difficult to comprehend. He remembers that right after war began, in September 1939, his parents drove the children to the Spanish–Portuguese border: "My parents and two of my brothers returned to Bordeaux to resume their respective daily activities at the consulate and at the university. The rest of us went to our country place in Cabanas de Viriato, Beira Alta, in Portugal. There I resumed my education at the local school directly across the street from our home." He enjoyed those days very much because he lived on a beautiful piece of land that had trees, birds, a marvelous view.

The family's country place was actually a mansion that came close to being a palace. It was encircled by a wall, and on a pedestal in front of the residence stood an enormous statue of Christ the King. The entrance was decorated with many flags—those of the countries where each of his children had been born or the places Mendes had worked as a diplomat. The impressive family crest—fig leaves and five pinions, two eagles, two swords, a lion—adorned every chair, had been painted on ceilings, in the library, on stationery, linens, the family mausoleum. The house had a private chapel and family cemetery. Inside the residence were drawing rooms, an excellent library filled with great books, especially religious books related to his Catholicism. There was a pianola, and two of the best Bechstein pianos ever made. It had ten bedrooms, six bathrooms. Nearby residents remember that whenever "Aristides do Passal"—as Aristides was affectionately called—came with his large family for a holiday, local children would run after his car; when the car stopped in front of the mansion, Aristides do Passal would toss handfuls of sweets and chocolates wrapped in silver and gold foil to them as he emerged from the car. They also remember that, whether or not he was in residence, a meal was offered from the kitchen to whoever was in need on Thursdays and that the door to the kitchen was never locked. A hungry person was welcome at any time, a cold person was welcome to enter the kitchen and get warm by the stove at any time. It was here that his many younger children remained as the war bore down on their father.

War first reached the Sousa Mendes family when Aristides' twin brother, César—who was the Portuguese ambassador to Poland, stationed in Warsaw—witnessed Hitler's attack there. When bombs began to fall, César took his family and joined neighbors in the cellar of their large apartment building, which served as a makeshift air-raid shelter. César—like Aristides—was a devout man, and he led his neighbors in prayer after prayer while death rained down from the sky. Once the attack ended and the all-clear had sounded, and it seemed safe to leave the shelter, people climbed the stairway from the shelter. They stepped into the street and saw that the entire street was rubble. Only one building in the square block was left standing—their own. It seemed a miracle to those among the group who believed in miracles. Afterward, the neighborhood thought of Sousa Mendes as especially blessed. As subsequent attacks began, people clustered with him wherever he went for shelter.

When the German army attacked Holland and Belgium and threatened France in spring of 1940, refugees immediately descended on Bordeaux. They were looking for means of escaping Hitler's grasping reach. Vehicles clogged all roads leading south, people swarmed onto every train running south and—many having no destination—simply camped out in train stations. When Paris fell to Hitler in June, more desperate people descended on Bordeaux, which had become the acting capital of France. César's son, also named César, came to see his uncle at the consulate at this time and described his arrival: "I immediately noticed a huge crowd of refugees heading in the direction of the consulate. The closer I got to the building, the denser the crowd became. There were lots of old and sick people—pregnant women who were unwell, defenseless people who had seen their parents machine-gunned on the roads by aircraft." Then he went inside the consulate. "Even the consulate offices were packed with refugees. They were dead tired, having spent days and nights in the street, on stairways, in the offices. These people could no longer relieve themselves or eat or drink for fear of losing their place in the queues. The refugees looked haggard. They were no longer able to wash, comb their hair, shave or change their clothes. In most cases, though, the clothes they were wearing were the only ones they had."

Aristides quickly cabled Lisbon and described the situation. He asked his government for instructions on how to help these refugees. The reply he received forbade that visas be given to:

+ Aliens of undefined, contested or contentious nationality, stateless persons, Russians, holders of "Nansen passports."

+ Aliens who were unable to provide valid reasons for entering Portugal and whose passports contained indications suggesting they would be unable to return freely to their country of origin.

+ Jews expelled from their countries and stripped of their nationality.

One day Sousa Mendes passed a refugee rabbi from Antwerp, Chaim Kruger. He and his wife and six children were destitute. Without a second thought, Aristides invited Kruger and his family to stay in his residence overlooking the port of Bordeaux across from the big warehouse. They did. Feeling great sympathy for Kruger, Aristides sent a telegram to Lisbon asking for permission to give visas to this sorry family to get them out of France. The reply received said clearly, unequivocally, that the answer was no. Regardless, risking censure, Aristides offered the rabbi a visa that would facilitate the Krugers' departure from the country that had now become so dangerous. Kruger's son Jacob and his daughter Ann remember their desperate departure from Antwerp by train and the astonishing hospitality offered by the Portuguese consul.

They also remember their father's reply to Aristides: "It's not just me that needs help but all my fellow Jews who are in danger of their lives."

Sousa Mendes was stunned by the rabbi's reply: The implication was heavy. Essentially, the rabbi had said, *I don't want your help unless you can help all the Jews in Bordeaux.* The unsaid rejoinder naturally would have been, *But there are thousands and thousands who need help too. I can't help ten thousand people, can I?* Could he? Aristides' son Pedro Nuno emotionally recalls the conversation his father had with this bearded man who was wearing a coal-black hat and a long black coat even though the weather was mild. "All of a sudden my father seemed terribly weary as though he had been struck down by a violent disease. He just looked at us and went to bed."

John Paul worked as an appliance repairman in the San Francisco area when he first arrived in the United States, then he worked as an architectural draftsman. When we met, he had come to a Holocaust event in Los Angeles where I was also invited. He was to speak about his father, whose name was no longer known. He repeated to me what his older brother had said, that after speaking with the rabbi that day in Bordeaux, his father had become despondent. Rather than eating his usual large lunch, his father had gone to bed. In written accounts, John Paul's cousin César picks up the story from there, since he'd entered the consulate after Aristides had taken to his bed. He noticed that "even the consulate offices were packed with refugees." He saw exhausted people stretched out across chairs, sleeping on the floors, stairways, and some were staying in his uncle's private residence.

In 1998, in a letter to Yad Vashem—the Holocaust Remembrance Authority in Jerusalem—Pedro Nuno writes about the time long ago with particular sensitivity to his mother's even less well known contribution. He wrote: "It is our duty to pay tribute to our mother. I realize that tributes to our father haven't made any mention of her. When my parents and I were in Bordeaux in 1940, the doors of our home were opened to many refugees, some elderly, some less so, most of whom were Jews. They settled onto our sofas and armchairs. Some even lay on the carpet. I remember that period very well and I have had many contacts with those refugees. From that moment on, our mother looked after not only her children but also the refugees who worried her. Irrespective of their origins, they experienced the generosity and altruism of our mother, who was already fifty-two years old. In many cases she assisted them with great affection, and gave them food and drink. When others came into the kitchen where we took our meals, she served them without ever complaining."

The consul's despondency continued for three days and nights. He remained in his bed, in his darkened room with the shutters closed. He refused all food and had turned his face to the wall. Years later—destitute and obscure, his many children scattered around the world since his career had been ruined by his subsequent actions and he could no longer afford to support them—he would tell anyone who'd listen that lying in that darkened room for those three days and nights he thought he'd heard the voice of God. What eyewitnesses relate was that after three days and nights, on the morning of June 16, 1940, Sousa Mendes got up and left the bedroom. His family was shocked by the sight of him. "He looked grave, his eyes had blue circles around them. His hair had turned . . . as white as snow almost," was how Sebastião Mendes described his father's emergence from his darkened bedroom in a story he published in 1951. Pedro Nuno echoes Sebastião and others who witnessed that moment. Pedro claims that his father in-

Aristides de Sousa Mendes.

sisted unequivocally that he'd heard either God's voice or a clear, directive voice of conscience as he lay in his bed for those three days and nights, that the voice had given him precise instructions as to what actions he was to take. And he followed these instructions.

After emerging from that room, Sousa Mendes immediately went against his government's edict and issued approximately ten thousand visas to Jews and others—like Archduke Otto and the Empress Zita of the imperial family of Austria; the Duchess of Parma, who was by birth a member of the royal house of Portugal, the House of Braganza, and more—who had fled Hitler's armies in the year 1940. Even as the Luftwaffe bombed Bordeaux, the consul wrote and signed visas. Factoring time and marriage and reproduction and further reproduction into this number who were able to leave France, cross Spain and get to Portugal and elsewhere due to Sousa Mendes' visas, approximately one hundred thousand people are living and scattered round the world today.

His nephew César has not forgotten the terror of the bombing of Bordeaux. Throughout, his uncle had written visas. He recalled one particular refugee, Charles Oulmont, who had taught at the Sorbonne and was also a writer. "He moved into my uncle's home. He ate with us in the kitchen and slept in one of the bedrooms. From the moment he entered the house, he never wore anything but pajamas. He lived in mortal fear of being caught by the Nazis—but his fear was justified since he had criticized the Hitler regime in print. He was immensely wealthy, had four potato sacks full of solid gold with him. In the hope of persuading my uncle to grant him a visa, he promised him half his fortune. My uncle turned the offer down, but gave him his visa."

On June 16, 1940, Pedro Nuno had seen a washed, dressed,

white-haired man emerge from his bedroom who announced to all present, "From now on I'm giving everyone visas. There will be no more nationalities, races or religions." In July 1940, after being stripped of his title—and with a threat of arrest issued by Salazar himself hanging over him—the consul was ordered back to Portugal by his government. Aristides de Sousa Mendes drove his red convertible first to his mansion at Cabanas de Viriato, then on to Lisbon. When he arrived, the Ministry of Foreign Affairs summarily dismissed him without severance pay. His pension was suspended. Legal battles followed that reduced Aristides and his family to poverty. He slowly sold off his possessions and property. In 1952, after his second stroke, he sold off precious antiques, his Bechstein pianos, sinks, pipes, assorted items from his grand house. In 1953, he sold the remaining contents of his house for 15,000 escudos. He eventually lived on the verge of poverty on a stipend given to him by the Jews of Lisbon and was forced to bring his family to eat in a soup kitchen, the Cosinha Económica Israelita de Lisboa. He was supported by this small Portuguese Jewish community center.

In a documentary made for Portuguese television by Diana Andringa, Isaac Bitton described meeting him at the soup kitchen, where Bitton helped his aunt, a cook: "One day I heard a voice behind me speaking perfect Portuguese. I turned round and saw a man wearing a black suit and a diplomat's hat, accompanied by his wife and several children. Impressed by his presence, I went up to him and told him that next to the dining room for refugees there was another room, on the left, for the Portuguese. He looked at me with a strange smile and said in a very calm voice, 'You know, we are all refugees.'"

Sousa Mendes' wife, Angelina, died of a stroke in 1948. Sousa Mendes died on April 3, 1954, and—in accordance with his wishes—was buried wearing a Franciscan monk's garb. Who could have known or guessed from looking at his photograph that under the expanded chest of this portly man with the pouchy face was a heart that had crossed a meridian of conscience; like a dormant volcano, something had erupted within.

PART TWO

What Slipped Through

the Fingers of Death

World War II lasted for 2,174 days. The precise sum of what was lost between 1939 and 1945 is incalculable. Even the numbers—civilian as well as military deaths—are not precise. Estimates are that 362,561 Americans, 484,482 British and members of the British Commonwealth died, so did 420,343 Greeks, 240,000 Dutch, 6 million Polish, more than 6.8 million Germans, 3 million Japanese (138,890 in the atomic bombing of Hiroshima), 6 million Chinese, more than 20 million Russians (among them 3.5 million murdered prisoners of war). Two hundred and fifty thousand Gypsies, and tens of thousands of homosexuals, disabled and mentally defective people were murdered. In total, in Asia and Africa, Australia and Europe—Romania, Hungary, Czechoslovakia, France, Austria, Lithuania, Latvia, Belgium, Yugoslavia, Italy, Bulgaria, Denmark, Estonia, Norway, Luxembourg—more than 46 million died. Six million Jews from across Europe died, a million or more of them children. The attempt to destroy the entire Jewish population of Europe is now commonly described as the Holocaust or *Shoah*.

Of the estimated 3.3 million Jews living in prewar Poland, 3 million were annihilated during the war. Poland became the central convergence and collecting point for transports of deported Jews from across Europe. Millions of Jewish people were dropped there, from trains that headed back to collect more human cargo and return to Poland. Raul Hilberg describes how "a man would step off a train in the morning and in the evening his corpse was burned and his clothes packed away for shipment to Germany." Six major (and many minor) death camps were located on Polish soil—Kulmhof, Belzec, Sobibor, Lublin, Treblinka and Auschwitz.

Gas was the preferred method of annihilation, leaving Polish soil soaked with Jewish blood like no other part of Europe.

Very little slipped through death's fingers in Poland. Yet a few of the doomed did live. Some even journeyed back to postwar Poland to visit their place of origin or that of their parents, as these two excerpts from Theo Richmond's *Konin: A Quest* recount:

Izzy last saw Konin in 1945. Liberated from camp in Czechoslovakia, he struggled home by train, horse and cart, and on foot: "There weren't many trains and they were packed, with people lying anywhere they could." Sometimes he climbed up the iron rungs at the end of the coach and stretched out flat on the roof amid the smoke and soot. "We were young. We didn't know about danger." What about luggage? "Luggage? What are you talking about! A jacket and a pair of trousers that we were wearing. No money. Nothing. Just me and my brother. The Red Cross kept us alive." Now, forty-three years later, he was making another journey back to Konin, this time traveling first class. Trousers knife-sharp creased, shirt immaculate, shoes polished, he looked as though fitted out in brand-new clothes.

[Izzy continues:] "It felt unusual, dreamlike, to be walking through the streets I walked through so many times before in my mind. I had the old town map in my hand but I had little need of it. I knew which streets would lead where, what vista would greet me round each corner, which turning would take me towards the river or the Tepper Marik or the park. Seeing the landmarks in the main street—the Town Hall, the Catholic church, the medieval milestone—I felt a jolt of recognition like a reincarnated soul returning from a previous life.

"I stood on Third of May Street, and opened the Memorial Book at the pre–First World War photograph of the Town Hall in what was

then 'Long Street, Konin, Russian Poland.' Long Street became Third of May Street, which became Hermann Göring Strasse, which was now Red Army Street. (After the fall of the Communist regime it went back to Third of May Street.) A few details had changed since the photograph was taken. A memorial to the Red Army stood in front of the Town Hall. Some trees had disappeared. But in most respects the view I was looking at—the white building with the pretty hexagonal clock tower—was the one my grandparents saw a hundred years ago when they walked along Ulca Dluga (Long Street) and glanced up to check the time. The streets running along either side of the Town Hall, the houses, rooftops, iron balconies in the old picture, were still recognizable today, despite the post-Tsarist incursion of a satellite dish."

But very few Polish Jews were ever to return. In Poland, like other parts of Europe, so much was destroyed in World War II, so much was obliterated. How was it possible that any remnants of civilization, of humanity or culture—of love, of music, of memory, of sentience—were able to fall through such a dense blanket of destruction? Could literature withstand the conflagration? Could theater? Could art?

THE SURVIVAL OF LITERATURE

And yet the books will be there on the shelves, separate beings,
That appeared once, still wet
As shining chestnuts under a tree in autumn,
And, touched, coddled, began to live
In spite of fires on the horizon, castles blown up,
Tribes on the march, planets in motion.
"We are," they said, even as their pages
Were being torn out, or a buzzing flame
Licked away their letters. So much more durable
Than we are, whose frail warmth
Cools down with memory, disperses, perishes.
I imagine the earth when I am no more:
Nothing happens, no loss, it's still a strange pageant,
Women's dresses, dewy lilacs, a song in the valley.
Yet the books will be there on the shelves, well born,
Derived from people, but also from radiance, heights.

"AND YET THE BOOKS" — Czeslaw Milosz

Literature did withstand the conflagration: Brought to Rome originally as slaves, Jews were known to live there as early as 161 B.C. They were walled into a ghetto in 1555, when Pope Paul IV sequestered a neighborhood close to the Tiber River in which Jews clustered. Subsequently—by the 1930s—the library of the Roman Jewish community was the most scholarly, venerable and valuable library of Jewish books in all of Italy and the oldest in Europe. In October 1943, the Italian moving company Otto & Rosoni was contracted by the German SS, as ordered by the Einsatzstab Reichsleiter Rosenberg (a team whose mission was the confiscation of libraries, headed by the high-ranking Nazi Alfred Rosenberg), to collect the uncatalogued seven thousand books contained in the Roman Jewish library. Estelle Gilson, a scholar and translator, discovered in her research on the fate of this library that many of the books were stamped with the library seal. "They were treated carefully—stacked in layers with corrugated sheets between—and packed in wicker cases. The loading operation took all day." The books were loaded into two freight cars, also with great care. Although little is known of the subsequent fate of the priceless manuscripts, incunabula (works printed before 1501), books and papers, methodical German documentation exists that notates that the freight cars containing the entire library were carefully marked "DRPI München 97970-C" and "DRPI München 97970-G." Then, as with the commonly transported human cargo, the freight cars were sealed shut. They began their journey to Germany, presumably to Munich.

Although 1,200,000 catalogued Jewish-related literary materials were later located outside Frankfurt in the town of Hungen in 1945 at war's end, and other materials were discovered subsequently in other hiding places scattered across Germany, the venerable Roman Jewish library was not among them. Unsuccessful searches were undertaken to locate the looted library, but the scent of their journey goes ice cold at the railroad tracks in Rome. Because like materials from Jewish collections were funneled into a storage building in Offenbach, it was thought that perhaps this cache also contained all or part of the Roman library, but after careful examination of a multitude of looted materials for repatriation, no sign of the Roman library was unearthed. At some point it was hypothesized that the two railway cars were destroyed shortly after their departure from Rome during the bombing at Civitavecchia. But no proof for or against this possibility was ever established, and there was no choice but to accept that the Roman Jewish library in toto, like much of its Roman Jewish human community, was lost forever. After the searches had come to nothing, it had to be begrudgingly admitted that Hitler and Rosenberg had succeeded in their goal of total obliteration. The value of this lost library—palimpsests, parchments, codicils, incunabula, papyri, commentaries on Rome in the time of Caesar—was incalculable. In 1945, when peace returned, not only had the culture of the Roman Jewish community been debased, all trace or vestige of its library had been annihilated.

But long after war's end, in at least symbolic mockery of Hitler and Rosenberg, a few shards were discovered to have survived: Estelle Gilson noted in her essay on the Roman Jewish library that the scholar Ariel Toaff had uncovered the existence of three incunabula from the Roman Jewish library that had eerily turned up in 1963. In the late 1970s, a further four incunabula appeared. During the examination of a safe in a synagogue, several ancient books were discovered. Buried in a garden was a commentary written in 1485. In a rabbi's office, at the back of a closet, were discovered several more incunabula. In the 1970s four more surfaced. In the 1990s, in New York, two books with marking from the Roman Jewish library were put up for auction. Although both the German and Italian governments—in renewed searches—have hit blank walls, at least fifteen items from the Roman Jewish library have somehow defied obliteration.

THE SURVIVAL OF
THEATER

T heater did withstand the conflagration: When Benno Meyer-Wehlack was sixteen, he was called to *Arbeitsdienst*—the duty to work. This was not exactly forced labor, assigned to prisoners and foreigners; it was something for German youth before they could enter the military. Here they could learn discipline and how to work—duty and work. It was the end of 1944. The red glow of fires from Allied bombings of Berlin could be seen on the horizon at night. Sulfur-colored dust was always in the air that smelled of smoke. Benno could hear bombs exploding even while he was below ground in shelters or in cellars and bombed-out, skeletal remains of buildings that pocked his neighborhood.

Benno had been living with his parents in Berlin. The schools were shut. There were lines in front of shops because food, even though rationed, was becoming scarce. In 1940, he had been evacuated to the city of Zokapane in Poland on a mobbed train filled with his entire school and other people. His parents wanted him back and he'd come back to Berlin in 1943. His father was a Nazi, wrote for a Nazi newspaper. By the time he returned, all schools were closed. He spent much time on his own except to help man flak guns with other boys his age. It was at that time that he got called up for *Arbeitsdienst*, received an induction letter into the military. Earlier in the war, before the Jews in the neighborhood had all disappeared, Benno remembers a Jewish boy blasphemously telling him that the war was going to be lost and that democracy would one day come to Germany. He didn't know what democracy was, so couldn't think about it one way or another. And—since all he really remembered was Hitler's times and the radio promising victory—he didn't imagine any other way. When times got harder and harder in Berlin, he wasn't concerned about winning or losing the war; he became concerned only about enduring.

Benno bid his parents goodbye and went as instructed to the induction center with a small pack on his back. He and other boys were sent on a very slow train to Sylt, an island in the North Sea. He was put into a barracks there. Because of the deteriorating condition of the war, *Arbeitsdienst* was no longer just for work but was suddenly for premilitary training. The idea was to get all young boys fit to fight. They trained with wooden guns. They were ordered to crawl across floors and to climb up and over difficult obstacles. Times were bad, he was hungry all the time. Some of the boys got packages from their parents filled with things purchased on the black market. But Benno's parents couldn't send him much. One of the boys had a copy of Thomas Mann's *Buddenbrooks*, which had been censored and was forbidden. One boy would read it aloud and the others would gather to listen. It was exciting because he'd never before encountered anything that was blacklisted. His father's newspaper had once been sent to Sweden, and a forbidden newspaper had been sent back with an article about a book by Klaus Mann, Thomas's son, who was also blacklisted. Clearly, there was a large world that had been shut off to Benno. The Thomas Mann reading seemed like news from another planet.

There were no uniforms available, so the boys wore ordinary clothes. Benno and the other boys had signed a pledge to defend the Führer to the last drop of blood. After signing, each of them was given a waistband decorated with Nazi insignia. A group of thirty or forty boys his age were then taken to a military base where there was a small military airport. It was next to the harbor at Rostock near Warnemünde. Here Benno was given a pair of pants by a mechanic at the airport. These pants were like knickerbockers, with the legs drawn tight at the bottom. They were mechanic's trousers, gray. At this base, although there was some discipline, no one took care of him. Benno felt inadequate to all that was expected of him. One day he came down with a terrible sore throat and could no longer swallow. He was hungry but he couldn't eat and began to get very thin. He felt completely shut off from the world and didn't have any idea what was happening in the war. One day he noticed that some of the military officers were moving out. He didn't know where or why. Large antitank guns were left behind. An officer gave these powerful weapons to the boys before he left and told them that they were theirs for their defense. Then he left too. At this point Benno realized that everyone had gone, that he was alone on the air base with a few other teenaged boys.

Benno saw two Russian tanks moving in a meadow, so he went into the woods and took off his military boots and put on civilian shoes that he'd kept, in their place. He got rid of his waistband and everything else that seemed military and then walked to Warnemünde. He crossed a river and came upon a forced labor camp, fenced in with barbed wire, just at the moment when the guards had disappeared. Benno met one of the laborers there who was dressed in white, a Hungarian. Benno thought he must be a baker. The man was undernourished and weak, hadn't eaten a thing in days. Benno decided to continue on and walked away from the camp. As he walked, he saw people coming in the other direction, trying to escape the Russians. He came to a market square in Warnemünde where a Russian soldier stood prohibiting people from entering. Benno told him, "I want to go home." As he stood facing the Russian soldier, trying to communicate, German Stuka airplanes began strafing the area. On the ground were Russians, in the air, Germans. Benno didn't know if the Russians would put him into a camp. They didn't interfere with him at all and let him pass the market square and go toward the ferry that crossed the River Warne.

Near the square he saw a small shop. He entered but no one was inside. Going farther inside, into the apartment attached to the shop in back, he saw food on the table, ready to eat. It appeared as if the people had just left. He didn't know where they'd gone. They'd even left their small dog, who nipped at him. There were edibles on the shelves of the shop, things he hadn't seen in ten years, like cherries. He was so hungry but—because of his throat—couldn't swallow. Instinctively, he knew that he should take food with him. He found a shirt and a jacket and took them also. From a bookshelf he took a volume of poems.

He knew that he had to cross the River Warne near Warnemünde to be on his way to Berlin. He reached the ferry and saw that it was still operated by Germans but was now under Russian control. It was filled with Russians who had swords. They had small horses—ponies with long hair, Shetland ponies—that were pulling carts. The Russians looked impoverished, not like a conquering army to him, but like he imagined Cossacks might look. He saw three cows coming on the ferry that approached his side of the river. He thought, *Maybe these Russians will kill me!* But he had to cross the river to get home, so he stood and waited for the ferry to arrive. When it did, he courageously got on and rode across. At the other side he asked the direction to Berlin. Someone pointed the way. A Russian soldier offered him a stolen bicycle. The Russians were cruising around him, having fun; one took away his coat, another his wristwatch. Today, a mature man in his seventies, Benno Meyer-Wehlack, respected German writer, doesn't remember anymore whether the wristwatch was his or whether he'd stolen it from the small shop. He recalls that the Russians offered him schnapps and vodka to drink, which he refused because of his throat.

He described to me how, farther along in his journey, he met a young German soldier in uniform who joined him. They walked together, speaking in German. That first night, they encountered more Russians, who took the German officer away, so the next morning Benno continued on alone. Because the Russians had given the foreign forced laborers permission to take whatever food they wanted, Benno sometimes at night joined the groups that gathered together in farmhouses, sleeping in hay. These former forced laborers shared whatever stolen food they had. For the first time he saw and tasted corn. He tried to avoid the main roads because these were clogged with traffic. Most of the traffic was going away from Berlin—west, toward the Americans—because people were afraid of the wrath of the Russians. Once Benno went to a house owned by an elderly couple and they offered him a bed for the night. To this day the memory of the ecstatic feel of a real bed elicits a look of deep pleasure on Benno's face. Benno remembers that the Germans he encountered along the way were anxious and terrified of what would become of them. People shared whatever they had with each other and with him. It was springtime, May 1945.

Along the way he saw that the Nazis of a particular village were being used as forced labor to remove barricades. After passing through that village he made a new friend who walked with him. The man was shabby, a German. He pulled a wooden cart. He was a sergeant. Around his neck, on a string, hung an alarm clock. It was his joke directed at the Russians, who were so fond of wristwatches. When Benno and the man would meet Russians, the man would laugh. The Russians would laugh back. The man was going to Leipzig. He told Benno that in his cart was his capital, he was going to start a factory. Benno saw that in the cart were uniforms. The man embarrassed Benno. They walked together for many days.

When they entered Berlin—at Wedding—Benno felt that he should invite the man home and offer him a night's lodging. But he didn't. At a street corner he told him, "I have to go this way," and abruptly left the man with the cart on the street. "For the next ten years," he confessed to me, "I felt guilty for not offering hospitality to this man." He saw that though hedges of forsythia blossomed in the parks, the city of Berlin was completely destroyed. It was a shock. Most of the shops and buildings were smashed into rubble, trams had been turned on their sides and were filled with stones. Sandbags were piled along the wide avenues. Everything smelled of gas. Some buildings still standing seemed to be on the verge of collapse, and whole streets had been cordoned off with signs: ACHTUNG! MINEN! Attention! Mines! Benno thought, *This will never be a city again.* He passed cooking stations run by the

Russians in which they cooked goulash. Goulash was a kind of stew that was new to him. The Russians were distributing it to the hungry people waiting with outstretched hands and empty stomachs. They were wearing shabby clothes, the looks on their faces were like that of people in a fog.

Because his parents had been bombed out during the war, Benno went to look for them in the place where they'd told him in their letters that they'd been assigned. But they were not there. He learned that they were alive but had been evacuated to Bavaria by bus near the end of the war. He wasn't unhappy that they were absent because he'd gotten used to being on his own and was looking forward to continuing his independence. It was an adventure now. He was invited to stay one night but no more in their former rooms among things that he recognized as theirs.

In the morning he went back to his old neighborhood—Charlottenburg—because he had to get a ration card, without which he wouldn't be able to get food. His throat was starting to heal and he longed for a potato. At the end of his street was a theater in which he'd attended plays with his parents. It was damaged but wasn't in ruins. Someone with a piece of cardboard was trying to clean some of the rubbish strewn at the front of the theater. He recognized this man as an actor from the theater. Benno offered to help clean up the rubbish and, side by side, they swept and scooped, lugged and cleared up debris. After the big debris was collected into a pile, Benno found two pieces of cardboard and began cleaning the smaller bits. He hoped the actor would see how useful he could be and would need him. He worked very hard, or, as he described it, "like a dog." Finally the actor laughed and told him, "You can be a part of the theater." From that day Benno lived in the semiruin and helped to make repairs. He was

Benno Meyer-Wehlack, 1946.

happy to be under the roof—or part roof—of a real theater, because he'd always wanted to be an actor. Other actors began to turn up and joined in cleaning and repairing. As a reward for supporting the Resistance, the conquering Russians gave this theater to Viktor de Kowa. He was to be its director. They also told him that he could open it.

Sitting in the living room, we drank strong coffee and stuffed ourselves on chocolate and cookies in the sprawling painting-and-book-lined apartment in Charlottenburg. This was the same building where Benno and his parents lived before the war, and where his parents would commit suicide together shortly after they returned to Berlin because his father couldn't find work and his mother had broken down. The apartment is on Mommsen-

strasse. He described how, a few months after the German surrender, in the first raw winter of peace, his father had asked him
to come up for a talk. He had gone, and his father had told him
not to visit for a few days, that he'd decided to commit suicide
with his wife, and didn't want Benno to be the one to find them.
Benno said that he bade his parents goodbye that day and—as instructed—didn't return to the apartment. Benno speaks rapidly,
always with thrusts of words and with wit. He shares this apartment with his wife of thirty years, Irena Vrkljan, an eminent
Croatian poet and writer. Irena and Benno work together doing
translations, writing radio and television plays. Benno insists that
even if official history always says that the Tribüne Theater was
the first to open after the end of the war, it was really his theater
that opened first and gave the first performance.

He proudly recalls his recitation of a poem by Erich Kästner
during the first performance. The first line was:

We were seventeen and we were scared.

Benno describes opening night: "The theater was dark. There was
a piano playing. I came on stage. As soon as I began to declaim, I
thought I heard the audience coughing but they were really crying. In the audience were women who'd lost their husbands and
sons who were my age, who sobbed as I recited. When I realized
this, I made them cry more, manipulated them with my recitation
because I enjoyed the fact that I was acting. I hoped then that I
could act and maybe write too, and live as an artist from then on,
that it was the route to moving others and being moved." Benno
was the only serious note in this performance. All were tired of

war and misery, they wanted to forget the past years, so the show was mainly cabaret. After the performance, one of the more seasoned actors took him aside and said, "You made it into a soap opera, an overdone thing. Please refrain from melodrama."

Benno lived in the theater for two years and took care of it as well as he could.

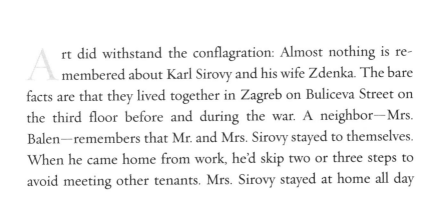

THE SURVIVAL OF ART

Art did withstand the conflagration: Almost nothing is re-membered about Karl Sirovy and his wife Zdenka. The bare facts are that they lived together in Zagreb on Buliceva Street on the third floor before and during the war. A neighbor—Mrs. Balen—remembers that Mr. and Mrs. Sirovy stayed to themselves. When he came home from work, he'd skip two or three steps to avoid meeting other tenants. Mrs. Sirovy stayed at home all day

Karl and Zdenka Sirovy.

playing scales on the piano. They'd rigged up—with piled boxes—a kind of protective wall on their terrace so that they could eat together outside but were hidden from view. Zdenka was Jewish and remained indoors during the entire war, hidden by her husband. Through the war they'd kept two vials of poison—probably cyanide—on their person day and night. They'd made a pact, in case the authorities ever came for Zdenka, that they would break their individual vials and commit suicide. Although the war ended, their tension and paranoia didn't end, and when the Yugoslav secret police came to interrogate Karl because of some complaints made by a jealous colleague in his office, he broke his vial of poison and swallowed the contents. Zdenka did as well. Then, when one body was taken away, followed by the second body, all their possessions—among them hundreds of paintings and photographs, as Karl had painted and taken photographs for thirty years—were confiscated and the apartment was emptied.

In 1979, Nada Vrkljan-Krizic, an art critic working for the Regional Institute for the Protection of Cultural Monuments in Zagreb, made an official visit to a woman who needed an export permit. On the woman's wall, Nada saw several paintings by Karl Sirovy. Nada would eventually become a museum curator, and I would meet her when I visited Zagreb, where she took me to the museum and showed Sirovy's work to me. We spoke of the Sirovys during several leisurely lunches. It was Nada who recognized the small handful of watercolors by Sirovy in 1979 during that work-related routine visit. She was elated by her discovery because she remembered Sirovy's work from her childhood. Her long-dead father had been Sirovy's friend, and three of his paintings had adorned the walls of the (changing) family residences throughout her childhood, the Second World War and its tempestuous aftermath. "Many of our possessions would perish in Zagreb, but my parents salvaged Sirovy's pictures, some furniture, some books and their broken dreams. The paintings soothed our loneliness. They were journeys into the unknown, figures with their backs turned; unknown faces; mysterious fates."

Sirovy's work had made a great impression on her entire family. In her father's diary beginning in 1924, she found comments on Sirovy:

> *I ate in a restaurant and worked normal office hours from six to eight. . . . I met people who will remain my friends for life at a place where I ate. They are a young couple. She is Jewish, a remarkable pianist, a capricious and frivolous little creature, very intelligent and well-read, exceptionally bright. . . . He became important in my life, and I liked him a lot . . . one of the most exceptional people I had ever known. . . . He is an artist in a real and profound sense of the word. He not only possesses an in-depth knowledge and understanding of art, but, as a self-taught artist, he paints small pictures, mostly watercolors, wondrously subtle and bizarre. He never exhibited nor did he permit his works to see the light of day. What a pity! When his works come out and become known one day, the art world will make a great discovery.*

Nada's sister, the Croatian poet and author Irena Vrkljan, who lives in Berlin and who introduced us, wrote in her memoir *The Silk; the Shears*:

> *Pictures from our former rooms also hung here; one was by father's friend Sirovy, who took his own life. It depicts a woman from the back.*

She is walking on a hill path, her red coat slit up to the collar, without a face, full of mystery. I imagined her with eyes closed, on the verge of plunging into a pit.

The father of Irena and Nada concluded in his diary from 1951:

This friend of mine committed suicide. He was about to be arrested. The next day his wife killed herself. I don't know what happened to his paintings, his books, or his work on the history of Slavs. I hope that they are O.K.—wherever they are, if they are. Dreadful!

After their father's death, Nada stored the three Sirovy paintings, which were bequeathed to her, her sister Irena and their third sister, Vera, as well as her father's diaries. When she encountered the six or seven Sirovys on that official visit in 1979, she recognized Sirovy's stirring work at once. "All the pictures had a similar whitish-blue-gray-greenish tone, as if it were a small cycle. They depicted men and women in groups, in long capes, mainly with their backs turned, in a forest. They radiated a sort of Watteau-like romantic atmosphere. My excitement was intense. I learned that Karl's sister Stefanija lived in Bjelóvar." It took until 1986—just in time because Stefanija died in 1987—for Nada to get permission to visit Bjelóvar where Stefanija lived.

"In 1986 for the first time I stepped into this hidden world. Mrs. Stefanija Sirovy remembered very little. She was almost ninety years old. She could not remember birthdays, hers or Karl's. She mentioned a few names of people who could help me find data about the family. I found these people and learned very little." Stefanija did, however, have ten pictures of Sirovy, albums and family photographs. Among the names she'd mentioned was that of Bo'ena (Enka) Gorski-Lovric. Nada wrote, waited. Finally a reply to her letter came:

The Weiss family from Bjelóvar changed their surname to Bjelic or Bi-jelic. They had three daughters: Zdenka, who married Sirovy; Zora, who married Gorski; and Zlata. Zora, my stepfather's sister-in-law, is proba-bly the aunt you mentioned. She was Zdenka's sister and she could tell you about this couple. Unhappily, you are too late. She died five years ago. I kept in touch with her until she died. Once we visited the graves of her sis-ter and her brother-in-law. She did not like him. She blamed him for lead-ing her sister to her death. They killed themselves together. I am writing to you because you are going in the right direction, but I, unfortunately, cannot give you any more information.

Nada searched for whomever Stefanija had remembered, in-cluding Mrs. Balen, the neighbor. Through a long search, much trial and error, she eventually discovered that Stefanija's friend Tomislav Cukrov had managed to save most of Sirovy's work—photos and paintings and personal albums. In 1992, she found Miro Vilcek in Geneva. He was Karl Sirovy's nephew. His mother was Zora, the sister of Zdenka. Through the many sources, art-works, photographs, biographical tidbits surfaced, bringing the number of watercolors and drawings Sirovy did between the years 1920 and 1935 into the hundreds. Nada describes these paint-ings: "He painted in the secessionist-romantic style, depicting the emotional and intellectual inferno of his soul and the unfold-ing pictures of dreamlands, phantasmal images and fervent senti-ments." Then she moves on to describe his photographs, mostly mountains, architectural shapes, overcast turbulent skies, solitary towers. "From 1935 on, Sirovy pursued photography seriously.

Watercolor by Karl Sirovy, *Blick vom Berg* (View from a Mountain).

During World War II, just as though nothing was happening, he continued to go on his mountain hikes while Zdenka ceaselessly played scales on a piano sequestered in their apartment. On these hikes he made landscape photos: felled trees, trees blown by the wind, an overcast turbulent sky, a solitary tower, a river valley, a bare steep cliff. The River Neretva, Omiš, the River Cetina, Mostar, Sarajevo—beautiful views caught by his camera." In Nada's continuing searches, the last photos taken by Karl Sirovy that were still unglued in the album were discovered. They were taken on Mount Sljeme. More paintings, photos, drawings done in India ink have been located. The graves of Karl and Zdenka at Mirogoj Cemetery have also been found. The first public showing of his work took place in Zagreb in 1987.

Because Nada Vrkljan-Krizic had not forgotten Sirovy, his photos and paintings have been rediscovered and preserved in museums, reproduced in books. Nada puzzles, "Did Sirovy have prophetic visions of the cruel, oppressive devastation at the end of the century we are now living through?" She points out particular photographs—some made in the '20s, others in the '40s. She explained to me that Sirovy went back again and again to his favorite mountains. "Nowadays they are just painful symbols of human existence, beauty-seeking, growing in the soil of their origin, today brutally devastated and ruined! He was a seeker of unreachable heights, of everlasting beauty. Multiple photos of his frequent trips to Mount Triglav in Slovenia attest to his admiration for the mountain. He was predestined for inaccessible peaks. He could reach them in his art and in his photographs."

THE SURVIVAL OF LOVE

I was with you in the mysterious gloom,
Walking as if in no-man's-land,
But suddenly the crescent moon
Skimmed like a diamond boat over the meeting-separation . . .

And if that night should return to you
In the course of your hidden fate,
Know that someone dreamt
About this sacred moment.

TASHKENT PAGES—*Anna Akhmatova*

Simon and Cyla Wiesenthal were ninety, still living in Vienna, when I walked into Simon's office at Salztorgasse No. 6 to speak with him. He'd just cut his six-day workweek down slightly in deference to old age. He had been fifteen years old when he first noticed a girl in his class in high school who had thick blond hair, beautiful skin, a soft round face, large gray-blue eyes, and was very, very smart. The year was 1924. She was named Cyla Müller and he was, at the time, known as Szymon Wiesenthal. They grew up speaking Polish at school and Yiddish and German at home. They were born in the same year, 1908, into what was then the great Hapsburg Empire, were subjects of Franz Joseph. The place was the small *shtetl*—town—of Buczacz in eastern Galicia, known for its clockmakers. It was then populated by Ruthenians (Ukrainians), Poles and poor Jews sometimes called *Luftmenschen*—people who live on air—because opportunity for Jews was so limited.

Simon's brother Hillel fell from a great height and broke his back. He became paralyzed and soon died. Then his grandmother died, and shortly thereafter his mother, who'd been a widow since Simon was six years old, remarried a man from Vienna. When his mother moved to the town of Dolina, close to the Carpathian Mountains, to be with her new husband, Simon decided to stay on in Buczacz to finish his studies. The town had by then become a part of Poland. His mother agreed. He took up lodging in the home of Mr. and Mrs. Müller, Cyla's parents. By then Simon and Cyla had become close; they studied and prepared for exams together, which sometimes she passed and he failed because he preferred making cartoons and drawing to studying. Everyone who knew them at seventeen had no doubt that tall, dark Simon Wiesenthal and small, fair Cyla Müller—so obviously besotted with each other—would one day marry. They decided that when he finished his studies, they'd do so.

Although Simon had a talent for art, he chose to study architecture. With so few opportunities available to Jews, Simon applied and was accepted at the Czech Technical College in Prague. This meant that except for occasional visits home, he and Cyla bore the hardship of separation for four years. In 1932 he acquired his *absolutorium,* but he still needed the equivalent of a Polish diploma to practice architecture in Poland. He went to Lvov (Lwów), Poland, where he studied for the equivalency and took a job with a company that designed and built houses for affluent Jews. Outside Lvov stood a tall wooden cross. In spring, garlands of flowers dripped from its beam because the locals never stopped commemorating the freeing of the serfs. Though he was far from established, Simon and Cyla were unwilling to wait any longer. On September 9, 1936, they were married by the local rabbi in Lvov. When one of the bosses in his company saw Simon strolling through Lvov with Cyla and commented, "Yesterday I saw you walking arm in arm with a *shiksa*," Simon could reply, "The blond girl with the gray-blue eyes is my bride."

In 1939, he received his qualification from the university and his title became Architectural Engineer, which meant that thenceforth it would be correct to address him as *Herr Ingenieur*. He designed, but when designing work became hard for a poor Jew to find, it was necessary for him to take a job working in a bed factory that made eiderdowns filled with goose and chicken feathers and bedsprings. Simon was able to bribe the right officials in order to receive proper passports for Cyla, himself, and even for his mother, Rosa, who—after the death of her second husband—had come to Lvov to live with them. In late June 1941, Hitler attacked the Soviet Union; by July 1, the German army had entered Lvov and renamed it Lemberg. Within hours, Simon personally observed that the assault against the Jews of Lemberg had begun: "I was in the apartment of a friend around eleven in the morning when we heard a loud screaming in the street. We went to the window and saw German soldiers and Ukrainian civilians insulting Jews in the street, dragging Jews from their homes, undressing and beating them. Two civilians and a soldier were beating six Jews with sticks. Near the curb, a boy of twelve or thirteen had been knocked down by a soldier, who was now kicking him in the head with his army boot. A few yards away two women were lying on the ground: their hair had been pulled out and it was lying beside them."

A Jewish ghetto was quickly established in Lemberg, in the neighborhood of Zamarstynovska Street. By the end of the summer, Simon, Cyla and Rosa were forced to move into it, sharing a tiny two-room apartment with another family. Simon and Cyla were sent to work as forced labor. In fall of 1941, they were abruptly separated—without time for a real parting—and forced onto separate trucks, he with men, she with women. They were deported to the sandy woods north of the city to a newly built concentration camp called Janowska, where they were given no more than three ounces of bread per day and made to do difficult physical work. Because of her age, her inability to do heavy labor, Rosa was left in the ghetto. Simon left his mother with the only possession of value that remained, a gold watch that he instructed her to use as a bribe if needed. By the end of the year, they and other young, able-bodied prisoners were moved into a smaller labor-only branch of Janowska camp, where strength was needed for railroad maintenance and repair, so food rations and mobility was much improved. This OAW (Ostbahn Ausbesserungs Werke) labor camp had no SS guarding the prisoners. Instead, railway guards kept watch and were sometimes lax in their vigilance.

Simon and Cyla counted themselves blessed that they were together and were able to meet each other, and sometimes after labor duties they were even able to visit Rosa in the city and stay the entire night. Once Simon came to see his mother and found the door open but the rooms empty. A neighbor told him that though Rosa had bribed one of the Ukrainian policemen with the valuable gold watch, a second Ukrainian policeman had rounded her up and taken her with others to waiting cattle cars. Simon rushed to the train yard, where he could see trains that were jammed with people. He has often said: "I knew my mother had to be on that train. The SS were guarding all the approaches. But I could hear the agonized cries from the trains stuffed with people. They were begging for water. But nobody could get near. A man told me that two Polish railway workers who had tried to take a couple of mugs of water to the train were knocked down brutally by the SS. I remained there for about half an hour. Then I had to go back to work. Next day the trains stood in the same place, the cries for water continuing. My only hope is that my mother died quickly, before she reached Belzec, the extermination camp to which she was being taken, and that she was spared the march to the gas chamber. She had a bad heart." She was sixty-three.

Simon would say later in his life that he'd had a terrible foreboding on the last day he saw his mother alive. But not wanting to cause her any extra anxiety, as he was leaving to return to his labor brigade, he merely gave her the usual rudimentary kiss and, without further fanfare, left for the work site, never to set eyes on her again. Not one photo survived the war. And—of course—no grave remains for him to visit to mark her passing. Soon after Rosa's deportation, the couple learned that Cyla's mother, who had stayed behind in Buczaca, was also dead. They were told that she had been ordered to vacate her small house by armed Ukrainian policemen. But because she had not been quick enough to gather her things, one of them had shot and killed her.

Simon's job was to paint over the hammer and sickles decorating captured Russian railway trains with large swastikas. Cyla also worked in the railway yards. She polished nickel and brass. Though they had been able to spend an occasional night together, that had ended after Rosa was deported from the ghetto and they were left with clandestine rendezvous at the Eastern Railway Repair Works through 1941 and for all of 1942. They were aware of what was going on around them in Lemberg, of the liquidation of the ghetto and the deportation of all its remaining population, that everywhere in Europe war blazed on many fronts. The Wiesenthals considered themselves inordinately lucky to remain where they were even though their meetings were dangerous and brief. When Simon's architectural and engineering skills were discovered, he was assigned work as a draftsman. The Germans had begun to plan a major renovation and enlargement of the Lemberg railworks. Engineers, draftsmen, experts were in demand and not easy to find because of the widening war.

A German civilian named Adolph Kohlrantz was hired to oversee the project. He began to use and then value Simon's drafting skills despite the fact that Simon was a Jew. Ethnic German and Polish engineers complained to Kohlrantz, refusing to work in the same room with a Jew, so Kohlrantz found an empty shack where he could install Simon. He furnished it with a drafting table and a telephone, and told him to work there; he said he personally would pick up and deliver Simon's drawings. Which he did. Shortly, he gave permission for a bed to be installed so that Simon wouldn't have to commute between the camp and the workplace. He was given permission to live in the shack, and amazed at their good fortune, Cyla was too. This began a period of—considering the circumstances—relative good fortune, compared with that of all around them. Neither Cyla nor Simon imagined it could last. Because Kohlrantz depended on Simon, he was allowed to move freely around the sprawling railway repair yards, and because he interacted with ordinary workers who were Poles, he developed relationships with members of the Armja Krajowa, or the AK—the Polish Underground organization—who were sprinkled among the workers at the railway works. Regardless of the daily privation, uncertainty and constant danger, each night he and Cyla would return to their little room and bask in the precious luxury of being together for one more night. Each day brought news of death, deportation, of sadistic treatment of Jews.

As was included in testimony at the Adolf Eichmann trial many years later by an eyewitness account, that winter for example— randomly—eight Jews at Janowska were selected one cold morning and made to strip and stand in a barrel of water. They were left in the barrel overnight. Of course they froze to death. "Next morning we had to cut the ice away." The same eyewitness testified that, in honor of the festival of Purim, six Jewish men were put outside the barracks for the night. "In the morning all six people were frozen lying down where they were put out the night before: completely white like long balls of snow."

Early in 1943, Simon was approached by the AK, who were doing preliminary footwork for eventual sabotaging of the strategically important railroad tracks, yards and junctions. They needed a resource for maps and someone with knowledge, and he was asked to help them in these matters. The Wiesenthals had of course been observing the systematic liquidating of the ghetto as well as the liquidation of prisoners in Janowska concentration camp. They'd noticed that the Germans were especially targeting weaker women and children. Simon has since said that he realized that with each passing day it was becoming less likely that he and Cyla would survive much longer. Regardless of his drafting skills and temporary privilege, they were both being worn down by poor diet and anxiety. Logic told him that at some moment their turn to be liquidated would come. Simon has always said that from the very beginning of the war he had no doubt that the Nazi idea was to eliminate each and every Jew from the face of the earth, so when the AK pressed Simon for a commitment, he said that he would provide whatever they needed from him on one condition. They asked him what the condition was, what did he want for himself? He wanted nothing for himself he explained. In exchange for maps and plans needed to blow the railroad yards and junctions sky-high he only wanted one thing, that arrangements be made for his wife to escape from Lemberg. The representatives of the AK agreed and papers were forged for Cyla. She was given an entirely Christian identity—the Polish name Irena Kowalska. She was instructed never under any circumstances to reveal her true name and her Jewish identity.

During a wintry night in early 1943, Simon and Cyla bid each other farewell. A trusted member of the Underground smuggled Cyla out of Lemberg to Lublin, where she was taken to live with the family of an architect who was willing to take her in. The contrived story she brought with her was that she was a Polish officer's wife and that her husband was a prisoner of war in a camp in Russia. In return, Cyla cared for the family's children. With her round face and fair hair, Cyla easily passed as a Pole. Nonetheless, though she was able to stay in contact with Simon through the Underground connections and even sometimes speak to him on the telephone in his shack, she lived in a state of dysphoria—for Simon, for the precarious nature of her situation, for conditions that were worsening daily.

To celebrate Hitler's fifty-fourth birthday in April 1943, fifty-four Jews from Janowska were to be shot. To further memorialize the occasion, it was decreed that these Jews would be professionals. But since only forty "professionals" were found at Janowska, the SS ventured out among Jews on various nearby work assignments. Three men fit the criteria at the Eastern Railway Repair Works. Simon was one. As a sudden rain shower drenched everything, all—men as well as women—were taken to a pit filled with corpses and sand and made to strip. They were told to fold their clothes and stand single file. Then a machine gun began to mow them down, one by one, in the heavy rain. Simon recalls little except that he knew he was going to die. He has repeatedly said that he remembers the slashing rain and observed the first four or five people in the line being shot one after the other as the machine-gun fire moved down the line of people. Then as through a fog he heard his name and an SS corporal grabbed him out of the line, telling him, "Follow me." "I staggered like a drunk," he recounts. The corporal slapped his face twice, before the shock began to lift and Simon was able to dress and return to his little hut where Kohlrantz was waiting. Because an artist was needed to draw a large poster celebrating Hitler's birthday, Kohlrantz had sung Simon's praises as an artist, and permission had been given to bring him back so he could design and paint the poster. Kohlrantz commented, "It's not only Hitler's birthday today, it's yours, too." The poster read: WIR DANKEN UNSEREM FÜHRER.

Conditions worsened in Lublin. Cyla had new cause for unease because the Gestapo had accelerated roundups of women who could not prove that they were official residents of Lublin. When discovered, these women were sent to a concentration camp called Maidanek. She deduced that if her papers were scrutinized, she too would be deported to this ominous place. Taking the risk, she took a train from Lublin back to Lemberg. There she hid for two days and nights in the ladies' toilet at Lemberg central station until her instincts told her that the moment was right to try to contact Simon at the repair works, dangerous as that might be. It was a mild June day. Simon was working at his desk drafting when a railway guard he knew knocked furtively at the door and told him that he should come immediately to the fence on the periphery of the rail yard. There, on the far side of the high fence, he saw his wife standing. She explained why she'd come, and as he listened he understood her motivation for abandoning her safe life in Lublin. Cyla was quickly sequestered while Simon went to find his AK contact, not knowing if they would help them again. They were in luck. New instructions were given to Cyla. And after barely a few hours together, she and Simon were parted once more.

Following the instructions, Cyla went back to the Lemberg central station and purchased a ticket on a particular morning train going to Warsaw. On arrival at the Warsaw central station she went as instructed to a designated place in the main waiting room and stood until she was contacted by a female member of the Underground who gave new forged papers to her. Once again she became Irena Kowalska. The Underground agent took Cyla as Irena to a small apartment at 5 Topiel Street in Warsaw, where she was given a bed in the kitchen, sharing it with breeding rabbits. Another lone woman lived in the apartment, but neither of them asked the other personal questions. Soon after her arrival, Cyla went out to look for work and was hired to work in a radio factory. All around her in Warsaw, Jews were being hounded and hunted and, when captured, either deported to a concentration camp or taken to the dreaded Warsaw Ghetto. Briefly, after her second escape, Simon and Cyla were able to stay in touch with each other. A few times, the contact from the Underground would see to it that messages were brought back and forth. Occasionally, she could telephone his hut and they could speak and reassure each other that they were both still among the living. That is, until October 6, 1943, when he learned that he was to be sent back to Janowska where he knew he too would be liquidated. Simon hatched an escape from Lemberg. Quickly he went into hiding and then he joined the Polish partisans hidden in the forest. At this point, communications between Simon and Cyla were cut off.

Simon remained in hiding until he was captured on June 13, 1944. Two pistols as well as illegal drawings and sketches were discovered on his person. They took him back to Janowska, where he had no doubt that he'd be tortured to reveal names of his Underground connections, and then killed. So on the journey back to the camp, he slashed both wrists with a razor blade he'd hidden. Word trickled back to the repair works that Simon Wiesenthal, the draftsman, was dead. But Simon wasn't dead. Slitting his wrists was only the first of three unsuccessful suicide attempts he made at various times. Knowing he'd soon be killed, he decided that he preferred to die by his own hand. On the first, he lost 2,000 grams of blood and was brought to the Gestapo prison hospital, where a doctor saved him. Next he stole and swallowed what he thought were a hundred lethal pills. But this failed too because he'd mistakenly taken the wrong pills. Finally, he tried to hang himself with his own trousers that he'd twisted into a noose. But this too failed. When he was brought back to Janowska in a truck with other captured Jews, the new commandant asked the prisoner, "What should we do with you?" To which Simon has said that he answered, "Please, shoot me." And aware of Simon's several failed suicide attempts, Warzok, the German in charge, sardonically rejoined, "No. A Jew should never die when he wishes, only when we wish."

Although the Warsaw Uprising was in progress, Cyla—as Irena Kowalska—went daily to her job at the radio factory. One day she was contacted by a member of the Underground coming from Lemberg, a courier. He told her, "Wiesenthal was arrested by a Gestapo man, Waltke. He cut his wrists . . . and is dead." Shortly after learning that she was a widow, Cyla was shipped to a camp in Solingen, Germany, with a group of able-bodied Polish women who were needed to work as forced labor in a machine-gun factory. While she was in Solingen, the building in which she'd been living in Warsaw—in fact, the entire street she had just left—was blown up.

On July 19, 1944, Simon and a small group of the last remaining Jews from Janowska were loaded into a freight car in the Lemberg train yards where he and Cyla had lived together, where he had heard the cries from a similar freight car in which he believed his mother had been locked. From inside, Simon could hear explosions from Russian artillery in the distance. He'd seen the German army starting to retreat and heard bombs falling. He, like everyone else, knew that Hitler was losing the war. The occupants of the freight car were fearful that they were to be gassed, but just before the train began its journey, a caged dog and a caged canary—pets of an SS officer—were put into the freight car with them. Simon later commented, "That was the best news because the SS men all loved their pets and would never be so unhuman as to gas them." The train stopped at the small city of Przemysl, then traveled on past Dobromil and on to a field close to Grybow where Simon's group slept outside on the ground.

Simon's group was marched to Chelmiec in September, then Nowy Sacz, then on toward Krakow. Finally, those still alive arrived in the feared slave labor camp at Plaszow, where Simon remained during the winter. Around the new year, he was relocated to Gross-Rosen camp near Breslau in Lower Silesia, where he would work in the quarry. At Gross-Rosen, Simon encountered people who'd been in Warsaw. Longing for news of Cyla, he persistently asked around for someone who might know people at 5 Topiel Street. Eventually he encountered a man who'd lived at 7 Topiel Street. Simon asked if he had news of an attractive Polish woman named Irena Kowalska. The man replied, "The blond woman? Yes, I remember her well." Then the man told Simon that Irena Kowalska was no more. How could he know this, Simon questioned. He replied: "My friend, no one in Topiel Street survived. The Germans surrounded one house after another with flamethrowers and afterward blew up what was left of the houses. There is no hope, believe me. Topiel Street is one big mass grave." When speaking of this terrible moment of revelation, Simon has gravely stated, "That night, I went to sleep a widower."

In January 1945, during bitter winter cold, a group of Jews that included Simon were temporarily shipped by rail to Buchenwald. In early February, also by rail, he was moved to Mauthausen, near Linz in Austria. During both journeys, the prisoners were crowded into railway wagons that were open to the elements. Dense snow fell so that when people froze they were covered with snow, where they remained like sculptures among the barely living. Of six thousand who started the journey from Gross-Rosen, only about one thousand two hundred were still alive when they reached the snowy stone fortress of Mauthausen. Marginally alive, Simon was in a condition of severe emaciation from starvation, with a septic foot that was swollen blue and green from the sole of his foot to his knee as a smashed toe had been amputated without anesthetic. He had already resolved that if by some miracle he lived through the war, he would be a witness to the gross atrocities committed in the name of Nazism. In Grybow, an SS corporal had toyed with him, had arrogantly asked, "Suppose you were taken on a magic carpet to the United States, what would you tell them? How it was in the concentration camps? How they treated the Jews?" Although the SS corporal could easily shoot him if he didn't like his answer, Simon replied anyway, "I would tell the truth." To which the SS glibly responded, "They would think you are crazy. They would never believe you."

The British liberated the Solingen camp in Germany on April 11, 1945. "Irena Kowalska" and a few hundred depleted but still functioning women in the forced labor brigade had endured. During the long process leading up to repatriation, Irena and six women (unbeknownst to each other during the war) revealed that they were Jewish and had survived by living under false identities with false papers. When asked about herself, Cyla explained that she was a widow, that her husband, also a Jew from the town of Buczacz in Galicia, which no longer existed, Simon Wiesenthal, a trained architect, had died in the hands of the Germans in Lvov, Poland. Discussions between Cyla and the repatriation officials ensued as to where she planned to go now that the war was over. She was encouraged to return home to Poland, to Lemberg/ Lvov, where she had lived before the war. Having no alternative plan or any home to go to, she agreed that, despite the fact that no one she loved was alive in Poland, this is where she would go. Among the survivors was a friend who was also going in that direction. After some time had passed, she and Cyla decided to team up for a journey east through the devastation and chaos left by the war, and they began their journey home. Though they were issued train tickets, there were no trains running. The two women began walking in an easterly direction. Sometimes they were able to hitchhike on a military or official vehicle. At other times they walked. Because of conditions of devastation along the way, they often couldn't travel directly and were forced to make detours. Among the many places they traveled through or near, one was the small Austrian city of Linz, known as Hitler's hometown but also known as the location of one of Hitler's cruelest fortresses, the concentration camp Mauthausen, which was just on the outskirts of Linz. They passed close to Mauthausen, of course not knowing that—very nearly dead, once a prisoner—Cyla's husband Simon had been there.

Weighing less than a hundred pounds, Simon and the few survivors at Mauthausen had been liberated by the Americans on a spring day, May 5, 1945. The survivors of Mauthausen were encouraged to return home. In Simon's case, the officials suggested he return to Lvov, since Poland was in ruins and no doubt architects would be in high demand to begin rebuilding. Simon replied, "Every house I built is gone. I have lost my mother, my father, my wife, and ninety relatives in Poland. Poland is for me a cemetery. Every tree, every stone would remind me of whole tragedies. How can you ask me to live in a cemetery?" Burial was a sore point for Simon. He knew his mother, who had died (probably by gas, then in all likelihood her body was cremated with many other bodies, her ashes thrown into a pit) in Belzec, hadn't a grave. He wondered whether or not Cyla had been properly buried. He said at the time, "I had no hope my wife was alive. When I thought of her, I thought of her body lying under a heap of rubble and I wondered whether they had found the bodies and buried her." He wrote to the Red Cross in Geneva who wrote back that his wife was not alive.

Soon after the war Simon went to the lieutenant in charge of war crimes and stated: "I don't know what to do with my life. I have nobody and nothing to live for, but I could find a meaning for my life by helping you with your work. I've seen a lot and I have a good memory. Men and women have been murdered before my eyes. I can give you names and dates and sometimes addresses. I can help you find the criminals." His life's work had begun. When the U.S. War Crimes Office was relocated near Linz, Simon, now beginning the arduous work of identifying, locating and bringing war criminals to justice, left Mauthausen and went to Linz. "We slept on cots in a classroom whose windows looked out on a small house that was the former home of Hitler's parents. They were buried in the cemetery at the end of the road. I didn't particularly like the view from the room and moved out of the school after a few days. I rented a modest furnished room on the Landstrasse in Linz. Not much of a room, really, but from the window I could see a small garden."

Simon began assembling documents and lists of war criminals, along with their crimes. He documented witnesses and victims of these crimes. Lists of the few survivors as well as the many dead were being assembled all over Europe. These lists were being distributed. Of course Simon read them. One of these lists contained names and addresses of the pitifully few surviving Jews from Krakow, Poland. Simon stumbled on a familiar name from childhood in Buczacz on one of these lists, a friend who'd become a lawyer whose name was Biener. Biener and Simon and Cyla had gone to high school together. Obsessed with the subject of burial and because Biener was a living link to Poland, Simon wrote to him asking for help. He explained that Cyla had been killed on Topiel Street in Warsaw, crushed under her building. But he hoped that there was a chance, now that the war was over, that the bodies of those left in the ruins might be identifiable. Perhaps Biener could investigate? Perhaps burial could be arranged? Of course sending a letter wasn't a simple matter at that time. Like the railroads, the postal facilities weren't functioning either. It was necessary for Simon to locate a courier who was going to Poland. And bribe him to take his letter to Biener.

Cyla and her friend left Solingen. They crossed into Czechoslovakia. At Bohumin, they discovered that one rail line still functioned. They squeezed into a car that would take them some of the way across Poland—now in the hands of the Russians who had liberated it—to Lvov. It was October 1945. There were many delays. Cutting through thick fog, the train reached Krakow in the early morning. A delay was announced. It would be at least four hours, perhaps more, before the train would move again. Cramped and restless, Cyla decided to take a look at Krakow. Despite the fog, her friend stayed with their things and Cyla walked from the train station into the old part of town. Suddenly, Cyla heard her name called. She turned and a face from the past, a man that she and Simon had known—Landek was his name—came out of the fog. They greeted each other. Their reunion was grave because Landek had heard that Simon had died. They exchanged other bits of information about mutual friends. Landek mentioned that another mutual friend, Biener, was living in Krakow.

In fact, his apartment was only a few streets away, up three flights of steps. He told her the address.

Biener had by coincidence received Simon's letter the day before. He was still absorbing the sad news that Cyla Müller, the friend of his youth, was dead. It was a foggy morning and he was at home when his doorbell rang. He opened the door. The shock of seeing Cyla showed on his face. "But you're dead! I just had a letter!" "I'm very much alive." "Yesterday I had a letter from your husband Simon saying you died when the Germans destroyed your house in Warsaw." Immediately, he showed her Simon's letter. What she felt at that moment, the revelation that the husband whom she'd believed dead for over a year was perhaps not dead, only Cyla knows. She has admitted that her first reaction was to not believe it. She told Biener that she didn't recognize the handwriting. She insisted that Simon was dead. Nothing Biener said would convince her. He begged her to stay with him in Krakow while they tried to sort out the truth. She agreed and sent her friend on to Lvov without her.

Then, Cyla and Biener wrote a letter to Linz, to the Jewish Committee. Because the Russians and the Allies had now divided countries between east and west, it remained difficult to send mail. To be safe, they wrote the same letter three times and began the task of trying to find couriers going west who—for a price— would include Cyla's letter in their cache. Some of these couriers traveled through Czechoslovakia, others went the longer way, through Hungary. As it turned out, two of the letters would never reach their destination, but Cyla and Biener had no way of knowing it then. The waiting began. One week. Two weeks. Three weeks. Meanwhile, still vastly underweight, frail, with a broken ankle that had been set, Simon remained sequestered inside his small room with his ever-growing piles of papers. Alone at that moment, he heard a knock at his door and a letter was delivered. It had been en route for five weeks. It was the letter that had been routed through Budapest. One glance at the handwriting told Simon the earth-shattering news.

Holocaust survivors seem to fall into two groups, those who never speak about their experiences during the war, and those, like Simon, willing to speak about the unspeakable. Fifty-four years after war's end, I sat across from Simon Wiesenthal, age ninety, in his small office in Vienna near the apartment where he and Cyla have lived together since a short while after they were reunited in Linz and resumed the marriage that continues to this day. Simon has dedicated his entire postwar life to justice. His leitmotiv is well known. In his words: "Justice not vengeance . . . to ensure that no Nazi murderer, however old he may be, will be allowed to die in peace." He has been willing to tell and retell his own wartime experience while Cyla has generally refused to speak about what she considers the unspeakable. I could not help but respect her wish to maintain silence and did not press further for an interview with Cyla. Cyla has admitted, though, that by being married to Simon, "I am not married to a man, I am married to thousands or maybe millions of dead." Both she and her husband have called their reunion a miracle—a word neither uses lightly. Simon has often thought, "If my letter hadn't reached Biener the day before, if Cyla's train hadn't been delayed, if she hadn't gone for that walk, if she hadn't met Landek, if Biener hadn't been at home, then the two women would have gone back to the station and continued their journey. . . ." There's no doubt that Cyla would have disappeared behind what would shortly be called the vast Iron Curtain.

But the letter *had* reached Biener. The train *had* been delayed. Cyla *had* gone for a walk. She *had* met Landek. Biener *had* been at home. And destiny would later give them a daughter named Paulinka nine months after their reunion and allow them to resume their lives together well into their nineties. But back in late fall of 1945, when Simon first held the letter from Cyla in his emaciated hands, a thirty-seven-year-old Simon, who—along with his wife—had brushed against death so many times he couldn't count them, had hobbled outside his room in Linz and over to the OSS office on a broken ankle. He'd insisted to his boss that it was essential that he go immediately to Krakow. The boss was an American captain named O'Meara who refused to give Simon permission to cross over into the Russian sector. Besides, he reminded Simon, he had a broken foot and couldn't travel anyway. He and Simon did, however, quickly hatch a plan to bring Cyla over to the American sector to Linz. Entry permits, travel documents, other paperwork were provided by O'Meara. An escort would be necessary to go to Linz and bring her back. Simon found the right escort when he chanced on a man originally from Krakow whose wife had been murdered in Auschwitz. His name was Felix Weisberg. Weisberg agreed to take on the dangerous task of traveling through Czechoslovakia to Poland to fetch Simon's recently reincarnated wife and set off while Simon anxiously waited.

Weisberg cadged a ride on a truck that was going almost the entire way. Unfortunately, as the truck waited to cross from the American into the Russian zone, he became fearful that he would be arrested as a spy. In a fit of nerves, he destroyed all the papers that he was carrying except his own; Cyla's papers were among those destroyed. When Weisberg safely entered Krakow he realized that he had no way of finding Cyla, since her address was gone with her letter. All the while Cyla had continued to wait in Krakow. Did she continue to hope against hope that her husband was alive? Or did that small surge of hope fade as the days grew short, the season changed and weeks passed? Only Cyla knows how she felt, keeping these memories to herself for all these years. The fact is that October passed and November was quickly passing. The harsh Polish winter had truly arrived when she became aware that on the Krakow Jewish Committee's bulletin board, a note had been posted: *Would Cyla Wiesenthal please get in touch with Felix Weisberg who will take her to her husband in Linz.* Details on the whereabouts of Weisberg were included.

Weisberg had found a room in which to stay in Krakow. After he had posted his notice on the bulletin board, three entirely different women presented themselves to him as Mrs. Simon Wiesenthal. Probably because travel papers were so hard to come by, here was an opportunity to travel out of Poland into the western sectors. Because there had been no reason to ask Simon to give a physical description of his wife and because Weisberg basically knew so little about either Simon or his wife, Weisberg had no idea how to decide which woman was telling the truth. He listened carefully to each woman's story; then, after buying forged papers for travel on the black market, he chose one of them to take and they immediately began the arduous journey from Krakow to Linz.

December brought snow and icy rain. The war had been over for seven months and the soft white of fresh snow had covered and made abstract the many remaining reminders of the war. Because of his broken ankle, Simon was in his room when there was a knock at the door. He was thirty-seven years old and still vastly underweight. On his desk lay bundles of papers meant to incriminate those on whom lay guilt. When Weisberg walked into the

Cyla and Simon Wiesenthal, 1936.

room alone, his heart must have sunk. But when Weisberg related the saga of the lost address and the three Mrs. Wiesenthals and that he had made a guess and chosen one of these women to bring, Simon insistently asked Weisberg where the woman was. And Weisberg replied that she was waiting downstairs. Simon asked Weisberg to please bring the woman to his room. And for a few final seconds, Cyla stood on a chilly white street in Linz while Simon waited in his paper-filled room, to know for sure and with their own eyes if lost love had really been released from the jaws of death.

THE SURVIVAL OF MUSIC

The first time Wladyslaw Szpilman played piano again after the war, he played Chopin's Nocturne in C-sharp Minor. Six years before, as war had begun, he'd also played this beautiful nocturne. Both before and after, he played piano on Polish radio in Warsaw. He was—as his son Andrzej much later described him—someone in whom music was alive. Szpilman was a composer, a musician, a songwriter, and became a celebrated individual well known throughout Poland. Like many survivors, he rarely spoke about his experience after the war, but surprisingly he decided to write of his experience as one of the rare individuals who had survived the entire war while remaining in occupied Warsaw. His memoir, titled *Death of a City*, was briefly published in Polish in 1946 but quickly disappeared. This memoir was translated and republished as *The Pianist*; it was brought to the screen by Roman Polanski.

Having studied piano and composition in Berlin in the 1930s, Wladyslaw "Wladek" Szpilman left his studies when Hitler took power because he was Jewish. He returned to his native Warsaw, moved back in with his parents and siblings on Sliska Street and was working as a pianist for Polish radio on September 1, 1939,

when Hitler attacked Poland, beginning the German siege of
Warsaw with artillery shelling and bombing.

In mid-September, the Szpilmans moved from their third-
floor apartment in with friends who had a first-floor apartment
on Panska Street. On September 23, Wladek gave the Chopin
concert. Then he went home. That afternoon he remembers
listening to a recording of Rachmaninoff's Piano Concerto in
C Minor on the radio. Toward the end of the second movement,
the radio went dead. In the afternoon he worked on a new composition. When the day ended, he looked out of the window of the
apartment and saw that fires were burning. He went out to have
a better look at Marszalkowska Street; Krolewska Street, Grzy-
bowski Square and Sienna Street, all nearby, were also in flames
and the sky above was filled with smoke. He wrote: "Outside the
door of our building lay the corpse of a woman with her head and
one arm blown off. Her blood flowed into the gutter in a long, dark
stream, and then ran on into a drain covered by a grating."

By September 27, the siege was over, Warsaw had surrendered
and the German occupation began. The family Szpilman returned
to their Sliska Street apartment where the father, in order to
block out the grim uncertainty facing them all, endlessly played
his violin. In order to avoid bowing down to every German soldier that he passed on the street—as the edict demanded—Wladyslaw stopped going outside of the apartment until evening.
Jews could no longer travel and Jewish money was frozen. The
family lived in hope that Germany would be quickly defeated, but
in spring of 1940, Holland, Belgium, Denmark, Norway fell, and
their hope of a quick trouncing of Nazi Germany faded. When he
heard the news that France had fallen, Szpilman's head bent until
it touched the piano keys and he began to sob. By late autumn,

transports of Jews to Belzec and Hrubieszow labor camps began and, in November, all remaining Jews were ordered to move into a confined and walled section of the city that became known as the Warsaw Ghetto. Although there was barely room for a hundred thousand people, half a million people were squeezed inside.

Wladyslaw remained in the ghetto until July 1942. In order to survive, his sisters Halina and Regina, brother Henryk and parents sold his piano as well as everything else of any value. Wladyslaw got a job playing piano in the afternoons, first at the Café Nowoczesna, then at a café on Sienna Street where Jewish painters, intellectuals and writers went. After that, he played piano at the Sztuka Café in Leszno Street, where concerts and musical performances were organized. Only the rich and intelligentsia frequented these cafés. But in the ghetto, among the poor, living conditions became so bad that an epidemic of typhus broke out. Five thousand people died from typhus every month and vermin infested the entire ghetto. He explained, "The clothing of people you passed in the street was infested by lice, and so were the interiors of trams and shops. Lice swarmed over the pavements, up stairways, and dropped from the ceilings of the public offices. Lice found their way into the folds of your newspaper, into your small change; there were even lice on the crust of the loaf you had just bought. And each of these verminous creatures could carry typhus." Since there was no burial possible for those who'd died of typhus, they were wrapped with paper and laid in the street, sometimes for days, until they were collected for mass graves.

Szpilman recounts his journey home through the ghetto when it closed down: "The streets were dark and almost empty. I would switch on my torch and keep a lookout for corpses so as not to fall over them. The cold January wind blew in my face or drove me on, rustling the paper in which the dead were wrapped, lifting it to expose naked, withered shins, sunken bellies, faces with teeth bared and eyes staring into nothing." On arriving home, his mother barred him from entering the house until she'd thoroughly examined every inch of his clothes and removed and killed every louse with pincers. And so the winter passed. Conditions and the desperate bartering, begging, scrounging, working for food worsened for all, especially the poor. When summer came, "resettlements"— deportations of residents of the ghetto—had begun, and people lived in dread of finding their name on one of the lists or of suddenly being rounded up by the police. Those selected were allowed to take possessions weighing no more than twenty kilos. Also they were ordered to bring all jewelry, food and water they would need for two days of travel. Despair dogged Szpilman. Expecting to be resettled anytime, he lay listlessly in bed all day. In early August, he watched as Janusz Korczak, the famous educator who ran the children's orphanage, carrying a small child in each arm, led his orphans along Gesia Street with an SS escort. He knew that Korczak could easily have saved himself but had chosen to share the fate of his well-loved orphans and accompany them on their resettlement. Although he couldn't have known then what we, of course, know now—that Korczak accompanied his children right into the gas chamber—Szpilman felt anxious as he watched the long line of children, accompanied by a boy playing on a small violin, march toward the deportation center singing with sweet, childish voices.

On August 16, the Szpilmans received their order to report. They packed their things and closed the door to their apartment. They walked together to the *Umschlagplatz*, the railway siding where people gathered. They waited for long hours in the boiling sun and quickly ran out of food; hunger and thirst grew as the day wore on. In the afternoon, they saw a boy who had a candy box hanging from his neck by a string. The family gathered their last bits of money, which totaled the price of one caramel candy. Using his old penknife, Mr. Szpilman carefully cut and passed around equal parts for the six members of his family. It was to be the final repast they would have together as a family. In early evening, a long train of cattle cars smelling strongly of chlorine pulled into the tracks, and the SS and the local police lined up on two sides, making a path to the train. Using the butts of their rifles, the SS prodded the crowd toward the train, loading car after car. Straining to stay together, barely able to breathe because of the overpowering smell of chlorine, the Szpilman family was pushed along the cordon.

As they came near to the cattle car Wladyslaw heard his name called out. He felt a strong hand on his collar that forcefully jerked him out of the cordon entirely. The hand—that of a policeman who knew and liked him—pulled him away from his family, kept pulling until he was behind the line of police and SS. He tried without success to push back through to rejoin his family, could see his siblings and mother climbing into the cattle car. He saw his father turn and search the crowd for him. He shouted out, "Papa." With all his strength he again tried but failed to break through the line of police and SS. His father caught sight of him. "He tried to smile, helplessly, painfully, raised his hand and waved goodbye, as if I were setting out into life and he was already greeting me from beyond the grave." For an eternal moment their eyes locked, then the old man turned and climbed up into the train to join his family, leaving his music-loving son pushing frantically without success against the policemen's unyielding shoulders. As Wladek shouted to his family, the policeman who'd pulled him away hissed at him, "What do you think you're doing? Go on, save yourself!" He saw the door of the train slide shut; he heard the train laboriously begin its journey. Only then—weeping, and for the next two years—did he begin to run to save his own life.

Wladek describes the beginning of his flight away from death: "With every step I took along the pavement I became lonelier. I was aware of being torn irrevocably from everything that had made up my life until now. I didn't know what awaited me, only that it was sure to be as bad as I could imagine." He returned to the ghetto but not to the family apartment. Although he had the possibility of a job playing piano at the German casino, he declined and began working as a laborer carrying buckets of lime, iron bars, stacks of bricks. Daily he was marched out into Warsaw to work and then back into the ghetto in the evening. He began smuggling potatoes and bread and eventually bullets and explosives back into the ghetto with him. The approach of winter caused him great fear because he had no gloves and he knew, working out of doors all day long as he was, that if his fingers became frostbitten, any hope of ever again playing piano would be dashed. Realizing that the ghetto was quickly being liquidated, he began without success to contact people he had once known who lived in Aryan Warsaw, hoping to find someone who'd be willing to risk his own life to hide him. Finally, a friend gave him a fifth-floor artist's studio at 10 Noakowsky Street with a camp bed. He took his only possessions—his fountain pen, his watch, his music compositions—and, weary and despondent, went into hiding on February 13, 1943.

Next, through music friends, he hid in a bachelor flat at 83 Pulawska Street, to which food was brought twice a week. This was where he decided that if his capture by the Germans was imminent, he would commit suicide rather than be taken. News of the Jewish ghetto uprising was brought to him along with his food. It was common knowledge that despite their very limited power, the Jewish Resistance was inflicting heavy losses on the Germans, who were battling building by building, and that—when all was lost—Jewish residents were throwing themselves and their children from the roofs of these buildings rather than be captured. Szpilman could see the light from fire reflected in the smoky night sky. In June, he narrowly avoided capture by the Gestapo, and shortly thereafter his contact stopped bringing food. So he lived on beans and oatmeal, making a meal of one spoon of oatmeal and ten beans a day, until that ran out. He lived on water for days, and, risking all, on July 18, went into the street and bought a loaf of bread with all the money he had and supped on it for ten more days until food was brought once again by his connection, who explained that the house had been under surveillance and, though they suspected that he'd died of starvation waiting for them, no one had dared to approach.

When a neighbor became suspicious and rousted him out of that apartment, he grabbed his few things and desperately went from friend to friend looking for, but unable to secure, permanent shelter. All summer he moved from place to place and finally managed the loan of a bachelor apartment in Aleja Niepodleglosci, a totally German part of town. The apartment was on the fourth floor. It had a padlock on the outside of the door, its key was kept by the contact who locked him in. Here he stayed for the next year and a half. He studied English and read all day long, in total solitude except for occasional brief visits when food was dropped off. The apartment had gas and electricity. In early December, he suffered a painful gallbladder attack and—again risking all—was treated by a doctor who was brought to the apartment. The new year—1944—began with a burglar's failed attempt to break the lock on his door. As the year wore on, Germany was losing the war on all fronts. Szpilman heard the sound of the worsening Russian bombardment of Warsaw and the beginning of the Polish rebellion against the Germans. His window looked over Warsaw. Bursts of firelight could be seen in the sky.

The fighting came nearer and nearer to where he hid. His food had just about run out one day in August when he heard the padlock on his door being removed, then sounds of panic from the other tenants in the building. From the window he saw a large tank and German soldiers facing the building. He left his apartment. From a landing facing Sedziowska Street, he watched as the Germans set the building on fire. He recounts, "So this was to be my death in the end—the death I had been expecting for five years." He returned to his room as smoke began to fill it. Feeling calm, resigned, Wladyslaw lay down on his sofa and swallowed the suicide pills he'd been saving for just this purpose. He was about to swallow a vial of opium he'd also kept for this purpose, but because he was so near starvation, the pills hit his empty stomach so quickly that, when he came to in the burned-out, smoke-filled building early the next morning, the opium was untouched. He woke to feelings of nausea, numbness in his limbs. His pulse throbbed. He had survived a night in a burning building. As he remembers and wrote, "My first emotion was not disappointment that I had failed to die but joy to find myself alive. A boundless, animal lust for life at any price."

Wladek was so weak that he could not stand up and—burning his hand on the red-hot doorknob—crawled out into the charred stairwell. He crawled down the stairway past still-burning doors and white-hot ash falling, over a bloated, charred corpse, out into the yard of the building, where he hid until nightfall. Gunfire close by continued between German soldiers and the Polish fighters as he crawled across Aleja Niepodleglosci Street past dead bodies into a bullet-pocked building under construction that was being used by the Germans for storage. Once inside, he passed out. Here he lived on discarded crusts of moldy bread and stagnant water in fire buckets filled with dead flies. He hid there as well as in burned-out apartments through August and September, into November, eating a few rusks and drinking dirty water left in bathtubs in deserted apartments. Allied bombings, artillery fire, and street fighting continued. More and more of Warsaw was turning into rubble and ruins that stank of decomposing corpses that were frequented by scavengers and looters. On November 15, snow fell. Szpilman now made his home in the attic of a burned-out building. Because the roof had partially fallen in, he'd wake covered in snow that had blown in. He saw his own reflection for the first time in many months and remembers it vividly. He saw filthy, matted hair and a black beard surrounded by black skin. His eyes were red-rimmed. Above matted eyebrows he saw a crusty scab.

Because German soldiers were searching the buildings, he again began moving from ruin to ruin, narrowly avoiding capture many times. Then, finally, while absorbed in a search of a burnt-out abandoned villa, he looked up suddenly and found himself face-to-face with a German officer. Exhausted, resigned to capture, Szpilman collapsed into a chair. He told his captor, "Do what you like to me." The officer interrogated him. When he asked Wladyslaw what he did for a living, Wladyslaw replied that he was a pianist. The officer scrutinized this starved, filthy wild man with

Notes from Chopin's Nocturne in C-sharp Minor.

disbelief and ordered him into the next room, where an upright piano stood. He ordered him to play something on the piano. Knowing that his life might depend on whether or not he could make music, he sat down at the piano. His filthy, stiff fingers with long dirt-encrusted nails at their ends touched the keys and began to play Chopin's Nocturne in C-sharp Minor for the German officer, who stood with arms crossed listening. He had no way of knowing as he began playing on that untuned piano that when he finished, rather than arresting or shooting him, the German officer would bring loaves of bread, jam, a fat, warm eiderdown and words of hope and encouragement that would keep Szpilman alive through December and halfway through January when—at last—he would hear loudspeakers in the street announce the German defeat. His salvation was as yet unknown to him. He simply played Chopin, describing the music this way: "The glassy, tinkling sound of the untuned strings rang through the empty flat and the stairway, floated through the ruins of the villa to the other side of the street and returned as a muted, melancholy echo. When I had finished, the silence seemed even gloomier and more eerie than before. A cat mewed in the street somewhere. I heard a shot down below outside the building—a harsh, loud German noise."

At the end of his memoir Szpilman wrote: "I sometimes give recitals in the building at Number 8 Narbutt Street in Warsaw where I carried bricks and lime—where the Jewish brigade worked: the men who were shot once the flats for German offi-cers were finished. . . . The building still stands, and there is a school in it now. I play to Polish children who do not know how much human suffering and mortal fear once passed through their sunny classrooms. I pray they may never learn what such fear and suffering are."

THE SURVIVAL OF SENSE

Though seen of none save him whose strenuous tongue
Can burst Joy's grape against his palate fine.

"ODE ON MELANCHOLY"—*John Keats*

To this day, Gloria Lyon, of San Francisco, speaks often and effectively at schools and for civic events about her experience during the war. She came into the world as Hajnal Hollander in Nagy Bereg, Czechoslovakia, in 1930, where her family owned a vineyard and farm. After the war, as a young woman in 1950s America, married to Karl D. Lyon, a lawyer, she explained to me on the telephone: "I looked like any other woman at the time. No one could tell that I was a survivor of the Holocaust. There was no way in my outer appearance you could know the turbulence I felt inside. Or that I'd lost my sense of smell in Auschwitz. Nobody could tell I had nightmares at night. No one could see the nervousness I felt bringing up my children." In 1938, Nagy Bereg became part of Hungary. In 1943, before the widening war had touched this remote place, a stranger had come through town. He brought news to the Jewish community of what had been occurring to Jews in Poland. The stranger claimed to have crawled out of a mass grave. He warned them of impending disaster. People thought the man was a lunatic, no one believed him until—on the last day of Passover in 1944—the Hollander family and all Jews in their town were ordered to a roundup. But then it was too late.

The night before the impending deportation, Mr. Hollander had been warned about the roundup. He called the family together. He told the children—Hajnal was fourteen—that in the morning they would be leaving. He showed each of them where he'd buried the jewels and other valuables so they would know where to find them when they returned. Mrs. Hollander baked bread for them to take on their journey. They sat together. None of them thought of the possibility that they wouldn't come back. At five in the morning came the knock on the door. The bread had not finished baking, was still in the oven, when the family left the house. The SS padlocked the door and sealed the lock with wax, burning the Nazi seal into the wax. The first time I spoke with Gloria, she told me, "Yes, I can verbalize it all, I'm a positive person. But I will never heal." She had been in seven concentration camps and two ghettos, Auschwitz and Bergen-Belsen among them. Though her family had been separated at one point or other, though they would never see each other again, her mother also survived. So did her father and her brothers Michael and Sandor. Her sister, Annushka, did as well. Only Gloria's brother Viktor—who was beaten by the SS and died—did not live through the war. After the war, all the surviving family members except Gloria returned home to Nagy Bereg. When they did, they found no furniture or livestock on their land. They did, however, find the jewels that were buried just where they'd been left.

In 1991, Gloria and her husband returned to Europe. They drove 1,750 miles in sixteen days in a rented red Suzuki automo-

Hajnal Hollander/Gloria Hollander, 1945.

bile. After arriving in Budapest, she reunited with her first cousin, Editke Karpati, whom she had last seen in Auschwitz forty-seven years before. Gloria and Karl then drove across Hungary into Nagy

Bereg that, since the war, had been annexed into the Ukraine. They went immediately to the Jewish cemetery. Although most graves were obscured with weeds and many gravestones were no longer upright because goats grazed and ate the brush, Gloria was able to find graves of her grandfather, grandmother, brother Jozsef, and then—precipitating an emotional outpouring—she found her mother's grave. She had last glimpsed her mother in Auschwitz. At the time she had no way of knowing if her mother would survive. Because of geography, they were never reunited after the war and her mother died in 1948. Gloria had no gloves, so she used her bare hands to clean the thorny outgrowth from her mother's grave.

Gloria and Karl then drove through the town. She recognized the house with two chimneys, where once a stork had nested, as her former home. She knocked at the door and an eighty-three-year-old woman named Ida Soter opened it and allowed her to explore the inside of the house. Gloria had dreamed of this moment for so long, had been anxious about meeting neighbors. She'd always wondered, "Did anybody shed a tear for us when we were taken away?" She walked in the neighborhood and recognized her school, houses of extended family and friends. She was greeted by teary neighbors who remembered each and every member of her family. "They told us how helpless they felt when the Jews were rounded up and how they'd accompanied the Jews as far as they were allowed to go." Afterward, she and Karl drove along the rolling hills and viewed what had once been the family vineyards, then they drove through the beautiful High Tatra Mountains and crossed the border into Poland. The next day they drove into the Polish flatlands to the town called Oświęcim. They crossed the rail tracks, the river, and entered what was the infamous death camp Auschwitz. They visited the museum, room after room filled with piles of eyeglasses, shoes, luggage, artificial limbs, hair, clothes, children's clothing. Then they drove on along the miles of once-electrified barbed wire that stretched as far as the eye could see.

At Auschwitz–Birkenau, Gloria stood with her husband, Karl, on the spot where the family had arrived in 1944 after four days locked in a cattle car with eighty people that had brought them to Poland. "We went through the gate of Camp C, the Hungarian Jewish women's section, where I spent seven months. I noticed the eerie silence of the place. The barracks were demolished long ago, only the foundations and the ruins of the barrack chimneys were visible over the abundance of weeds and wild flowers." She added, "We retraced the course I had to march each day." She stood on the spot where Dr. Josef Mengele—the tall German doctor wearing white gloves—had separated the men and women, where she had watched her brothers and father sent off with the other men. Her twelve-year-old sister, Annushka, had been ordered to go with a group of children and elderly, but she jumped off the back of the wagon when it passed Gloria and their mother. "We found out later that this act saved her life, because all those children were immediately murdered in the gas chambers."

Gloria and Karl walked to the place where the women were marched after the separation from the men, where she was issued a light gray uniform and her head was shaved—"I cried for my two long braids." This was where A-6374 was crudely tattooed on her forearm. "I worked about twenty-five feet from the gas chambers and Crematorium Number Four, sorting clothes, luggage, eyeglasses, dentures, hair, jewelry, wedding bands and other belongings into piles," she recalled. "The nearby gas chamber building wasn't noise-proofed and I was very sensitive to the screams of the victims, especially the cries of the children. I kept throwing up. Although we were given very little food, what was given, I couldn't keep in my stomach. I think it was from the putrid smell—the stench of burnt bodies—around the crematorium that had caused my nausea. My mother was very worried that I would starve. Then, one day, I lost my sense of smell entirely. I guess my body protected me. I was able to go on working."

Gloria showed her husband the place where her barrack had been, the place where, finally, she actually was selected and was wrenched away from her mother. "I could not say the word 'mother' for many decades after our separation. I was sent with thirty other women and girls to one side. We were all naked. We were put into a dark barrack, then a truck came to take us away. There were two guards. One of them came back to adjust the tarp. He told us, 'As you know, you are going to the gas chamber. If you want to jump off the truck, don't give me away. If you do, then both you and I will be shot and I won't be able to help anyone else.' He closed the canvas, went back to the front of the truck and drove off. The gas chambers were quite a distance away. I knew the road. I thought, *If I stay I will be killed. If I jump, I might be found. I might see my mother again.* I asked, 'Who will come with me?' No one answered. Again I thought, *I have my mother and sister.* I decided to take the jump.

"I knew there was a ditch at the side of the road. I jumped. It was night. I slid down an embankment, my body sticking to the ice on the side. The ditch ran into a culvert. I crawled into it. Soon afterward, I heard sirens blaring, followed by German voices on the road above. I thought they were probably looking for me. I stayed in the culvert all night and until the following night. I was naked, with no food or clothing in winter. I don't remember any feeling except a feeling of triumph, as if I had defeated the entire

German army. I don't remember the cold. The next night, in the dark, I climbed up to the road. I saw a tiny light in the distance. I followed the light, not knowing if it would lead me to the SS. It looked like a star. It led me—God led me—into a women's barrack. I climbed up to the third tier. A girl woke and screamed, I must have been ice cold. I put my hand over her mouth and explained what had happened. She took off the overcoat she had on and draped it around me. She was Czech. I have a picture of her. We were liberated together. The next day we found another overcoat on a dead person. I melted into the group. I was elated to be alive. I told myself, *Maybe I will see my mother again!*"

Next Gloria took Karl to look for the place where she had jumped off the truck. She doubted she'd find the hiding place, but discovered that the road was still there. She recognized the road, the ditch. But now the area was overgrown with weeds and shrubs as tall as she was, with rotted foliage untouched for over forty years. Then there had not been a blade of grass, now it was a mass of dark green vegetation. Fighting through the weeds and tangled brush, Gloria actually was able to find and uncover the culvert. She saw that it was a brick, semicircular drainpipe. She showed Karl where she'd once hidden naked in winter. She climbed inside and crouched down as she had done that winter night so long ago. Then Gloria showed Karl where the gas chamber and the crematorium had been and where she had worked sorting things close by; where she heard the bloodcurdling screams of the children and had totally lost her sense of smell.

This was enough. They turned their backs to Auschwitz–Birkenau and drove along the highway toward the Czech border. Their plan was to visit Prague during Yom Kippur and attend services at the famous Altneushul—the Old-New Synagogue, built in 1270—and to visit the Jewish cemetery where Jews had been buried, sometimes six deep, since 1439. They drove about an hour past green fields. The land was peaceful, green, flat. Gloria could not believe the contrast between past and present. "As we were driving through the Polish countryside, I said to Karl, 'What is that I smell? Is that manure?' Karl looked at me strangely. He pulled the car off the road and reached in back and opened his travel bag. He took out his after-shave and held it under my nose. 'Can you smell this?' he asked. I could. For the first time in forty-seven years I was able to smell again. My sense of smell had returned."

THE SURVIVAL OF MEMORY

Once it was believed in Europe that there existed in the exotic and magical South Seas sponges from under the sea that had very special attributes. Information, sound, stories, music, life experience that was spoken in the presence of the sponge was somehow stored within it and would remain there. Later—it didn't matter how much later—days or centuries later—when the sponge was squeezed, the stored memory could be released. Regardless of distortions of time, distance or space, the human memory would be preserved.

Her husband, Stefan, had been deported to Auschwitz, her mother, Stefania, had been deported to Treblinka, Adina Blady Szwajger, a twenty-six-year-old pediatrician working in the children's hospital in the Warsaw Ghetto with starving, disease-ridden children, was exhausted and soul-sick. She wrote in 1943:

TO OUR FRIENDS ACROSS THE SEA

We know, brother—
A storm rends the night, trees rustle—
You bury your face in your hands,
Ghosts beat at your windows and doors,
All your beloved ones have perished—
You alone survive.

Finally, Warsaw was liberated by the Red Army on January 17, 1945. Adina put this and other poems she'd written away. She began to work with the Main Committee of Polish Jews to find the few children who had been hidden with Aryan families during the war and who had survived.

After completing this work—in May of 1945—she moved from Warsaw to the town of Lagiewniki, close to Lodz. She'd been offered a job and took it. The job was at a TB sanatorium, where she worked with Dr. Anna Margolis, who had known her when she had been head of the TB ward in the Bersohn and Bauman Hospital in the Warsaw Ghetto during the war. Adina immersed herself in her specialization, diseases of the chest, and eventually married Wladyslaw Swidowski, who, as Wik Slawski, a member of the Resistance, had become her lover late in the war. He had helped people from the Warsaw Ghetto—and Adina—escape through the sewers of the Old Town to the center of Warsaw during the infamous uprising of the Warsaw Ghetto. In those first years after the war, she studied, secured the medical diploma she'd never officially received because of the war and decided to specialize in TB in children. She would work exclusively with children, as she'd done during the war, from then on.

Having already put her wartime poems and all memory of war years away, Adina decided never to write or speak about those times. And she never did. She explains her thinking: "If I remained silent, I'd manage to forget at least some of it and be able to live like everybody else. Years were passing. I didn't manage to forget but I still believed that I had the right to remain silent." She stuck to her vow. Slowly the bombed-out ruins of Poland were cleared and rebuilding began, the sound of hammering could be heard, the smell of fresh paint permeated the air. Trolleys again ran through the streets, damaged historic buildings underwent the long process of restoration or were completely brought down; rubble was cleared. Street lamps were replaced and the streets were lit at night after years of darkness. Eventually, one could find toothbrushes and even sour cream in the shops. To be able to add a dollop of sour cream to beet soup or to the top of a potato pancake was an exquisite joy. Life—days, then years, then decades—took on a peaceful cadence.

Her work as a doctor continued. "Being a doctor sets you apart from normal life. It means that you always have to think of other people's pain as though it is something more important

Adina Blady Szwajger.

than your own." Work, the hospital, quiet home life, became a kind of parapet set apart from the world. Forty-three years—a lifetime—passed. At age seventy-one, Adina became very ill. She was taken to the hospital and put into a ward where she hovered between life and death. She was tired of life and had no fear of death. Although her body was wracked by illness, the thread of physical life continued to hold her to the world.

For a long time, lying in the ward, she was neither dead nor alive. During this nether time, the memories she'd tried to kill hovered. Suddenly she felt that she was "in the presence of the past." Against her will, recollection and memory stirred. The image on a yellowed board that she'd painted in childhood came back to her. It was of her child's room, of a potted amaryllis standing on a windowsill. She remembered the view of rooftops that could be seen through that window. The painting was one of the only remnants she'd been able to preserve from her past. She called the painting "A Fragment of a Dead World." She remembered how she stood in a throng of people watching the conquering German army march along Krakowskie Przedmiescie Street, seeing the eyes of the conquerors that seemed to be made of ice. She remembers the taste of the half-pound of Pluto's chocolate she and her mother frivolously bought that day with the last of their money. She recalled the presence of fear that had to be hidden. "But it was there, coiled up tight, like a spring in your stomach. It would sometimes awake and send a piercing, icy shiver through your whole body." Images, fragments, scenes, gruesome memories of that time past returned. Unstoppable.

Weak as she was, lying in the hospital ward, dying in fact and not fighting against the abyss of death, Adina resisted the onslaught of memories but couldn't any longer stop them. They first seeped into her mind, steeped themselves in the waking/sleeping, conscious/unconscious atmosphere. Finally, the poisonous snake of memory bit through her strong will, releasing its venom. "Another fear came over me. That I wouldn't make it in time. That I wouldn't repay the debt I owed to those times." Suddenly, Adina feared that she would die without bearing witness to what she had seen; that her knowledge of the past would die with her. She called for a pen, for paper. "And I started to hurry. There, on a hospital bed, I started to write. Quickly. To win the race against time." Using the venomous memory as ink, though very late in life, she wrote a memoir that she titled *I Remember Nothing More: The Warsaw Children's Hospital and the Jewish Resistance*, which she was able to complete and see published in 1988. Although infirm, aged and not long for the world, Adina built a monument to memory using words as mortar. She wrote in part:

> *There's no trace, in this great, modern city, of what happened here. Yes, there is a monument. But not even a single fragment remains of the wall which separated one third of the residents from the rest: not a vestige of the stone desert which they made of the place where people lived, fought and died—people who had been there for a thousand years. Not a single burnt-down house from whose windows mothers had thrown their children and jumped after them.*
>
> *Sometimes I walk through that new, modern neighborhood, along pavements which cover the bones of those who were burnt there. I look up at the sky, there where my house and all the other houses once stood. When I close my eyes, the streets become familiar again. A crowd of people—shadows—wander among the shadows of houses and, clearly, as if they were real, I hear the voices of children, crying in that other language:* Hob rachmunes! *Have mercy! . . . Sometimes I come to*

Sienna or Sliska Street. I look at the hospital gate, peer through the railings and see that the Paradise apple trees that used to blossom there have gone. The hospital does not bear the name it should. . . . But I close my eyes. And the gate opens—the one on Sliska Street where once a homeless child had stripped naked—and all the people who have disappeared pass through it. . . . There is the Head Doctor, in her white gown, doing her last rounds, and behind her the doctors, nurses and orderlies, then the administrator and Dr. Kroszczor, who carefully closes the gate behind him. . . . I know that they've left everything as it should be and that Dola Keilson has swept all the floors . . .

Born Zahava Goldstein-Rosen, Zahava Bromberg has rarely spoken Polish—the language of her youth—for more than fifty years. She remembers the language very well but does not use it. She has dreamed about her past. The dream takes place in Poland. In it, she's walking down Brodzinskiego Street in Krakow. She walks toward her old house at No. 3 Brodzinskiego, reaches the front door. She stops. She speaks to herself, asks herself, *Can I go in?* She decides to knock on the door. She does. There's no answer. She's had this dream several times over the course of sixty years but never goes inside the house. She wants to go inside but at the same time doesn't want to go inside. It's the same with Poland. She wants to go back sometime for a visit, has always wanted to go back, but doesn't want to go back, has never gone back. She knows no one in Poland anymore.

Fifty-nine close members of her family perished in the war. Zahava survived and went to Israel. So did two other members of her large family. Her brother moved to New York after the war, her sister to Montreal. She, her mother, father—who owned two small stores, was so well-established and successful that the family lived in a luxurious house—five sisters and brothers, were all taken to the Krakow Ghetto on March 20, 1941. One brother was already married and lived in a town close by. He and his pregnant wife ran away to the east and returned a month later for the birth of their daughter. Before they were sent to the crematorium at Belzec, they sent this little daughter to Zahava's family at the Krakow Ghetto, hoping unsuccessfully to save her from death. In the ghetto, the family lived in one room with her mother's sister and her children, eating only a kind of porridge or grain and potatoes, getting hungrier and hungrier, until December 4, 1942. Her father cleaned the streets and Zahava and her sister worked near the airport as cleaning women and in agriculture. After a while, Zahava and her sister began living in the Racowice–Krakow Airport but were able to visit the family in the ghetto once a week. She remembers: "One day I came to see my brother at his work. He looked very bad. He wasn't shaved. I asked him, 'How are my parents?' And he said, 'Everything is okay.' But I saw that his shirt was ripped. I asked him to give it to me to sew. Then he started crying. I didn't know that this—rending of clothing—was the sign that someone had died. I thought that my brother's small daughter had died. He said that nobody survived. They all died, almost all of our family. I couldn't believe it, that five souls had died in a second; they were shot. They all died. I remember that I told my brother, 'Just don't ask me to believe in God right now.' Soon afterward, he too was deported to Mauthausen concentration camp in Austria, which he survived, and we"—she and her sister—"were deported to a concentration camp called Plaszow, where I worked in a factory knitting socks for the German army, and then to Auschwitz, where I worked very hard and was tattooed with number A-26495. And finally to Bergen-Belsen concentration camp."

Zahava was liberated from Bergen-Belsen on April 15, 1945, but stayed on as a Displaced Person. She went to school there and earned a high school certificate. Here she met and fell in love with her teacher, David, who was a soldier of the Jewish Brigade in the British army. David had fought against Germany on the Italian front, and after the war volunteered to stay with the Jewish survivors in Bergen-Belsen and teach them. David and other soldiers of the Jewish Brigade gave their passports and identities to survivors. In March 1947, she went by train to Marseilles, then sailed on the *Providence* for what would become Israel, where she would be able to study and eventually become a teacher. She turned her back on Europe. She explained to me: "I didn't want to be singled out anymore for being a Jew. I didn't want to see another sign on a shop window that said, *Don't buy from Jews.* Where could a new life be made? There was only one answer. I became a staunch idealist. Israel was the answer."

It took seven days for the ship to reach the port of Haifa. Zahava has since endured six wars in Israel, as well as all that has happened recently. She comments: "The first time I dreamed in Hebrew, I felt closer to my goal of becoming Israeli than ever before." She remembers the arrival. "On April 12, 1947, we docked at Haifa at night. Instead of leaving the boat immediately, my comrades and I decided to spend the last night aboard the ship so that we could see Haifa by sunrise and enter our new homeland by sunrise." She adds, "I have never wanted to leave Israel." Zahava and David, who was also of Polish descent, decided to marry in 1948. At her wedding, David's entire family attended. Zahava had no one, was totally alone on her wedding day. "I felt the loss of my family very strongly that day."

David and Zahava had a little girl together in 1950. In 1955, at the age of thirty-four, David suddenly died. She and her daughter were in total shock and remained alone for many years until Zahava married Arie, a widower with two children. "Today I have nine lovely and adorable grandchildren who give me a lot of joy, hope, belief and optimism."

Zahava Bromberg was born in Krakow on the street in the dream—Brodzinskiego Street. Her parents were Orthodox Jews, her family was large, her home happy. They spoke Polish. She recently told me: "Despite the tragedy and the suffering, I am not a depressive person. On the contrary, I am very optimistic. I inherited my optimism from my mother, who, even during the most dreadful times, told us small and terrified and crying children, 'Don't worry, kids, war is like a black cloud in the sky which soon will pass and the sun will shine again and beautiful, shiny days await us all.'"

She returned to the story of her wartime experience: "I was taken to Auschwitz with my older sister in October of 1944. Everyone was ordered to strip naked and discard his or her possessions. It was absolutely forbidden to keep anything personal." Against regulations, Zahava had taken a photo of her mother on the journey with her. "I couldn't bear to part with it. They would have put a bullet through my head if they found it. I tore off the image of my mother's face and put it under my foot, where it stuck, undetected. We were told to run. We had to pass the selection with Mengele, left or right. That would change one's destiny."

Where did the courage to risk her life to preserve the memory of her mother come from? I asked her. "From instinct," she responds quickly, then continues telling her story. "Next we were ordered to the showers to be washed. So that the photograph wouldn't get wet in the shower, I managed to cover it and put it in

The fragment of a photograph of Zahava Bromberg's mother.

my mouth. I kept it there, hidden. It remained relatively undam-aged." Of course they would have killed her if they'd discovered the preserved memory—one small photo of her mother's face torn out of a larger snapshot—hidden on her person.

"I was very weak after the Death March from Auschwitz to Bergen-Belsen in January 1945. At the gates of Bergen-Belsen, I threw out my blanket. It felt so heavy I couldn't carry it anymore. There we didn't work. We all slept on the floor in lines. To our luck, we were in the line close to the window—that was the best. The worse thing was to get rid of the lice. They were eating us away. Next to me were sitting a lot of Hungarian women. No mat-ter what we talked about, it always ended in talk about food. There I had a dream that my father told me, 'Hang on. It's not go-ing to last long.' One day someone came and said that there are no guards and the gates are open. When I went out, I saw peo-ple digging and we found sweet potatoes. We saw that the British were taking the Germans and capturing them. I took a stone to throw at a German soldier but I couldn't because the stone was too heavy for me to hold.

"The British soldiers who liberated Bergen-Belsen gave us cans of meat. Being so young, I didn't know that after long starvation I shouldn't eat the can all at once. I ate it all and became sick and vomited and couldn't eat anything. I was hospitalized. I weighed twenty-six kilos only. Suddenly we had mattresses and showers to get rid of all the lice. At the hospital, I met Erica, a wonderful English woman who took care of me and wanted me to go with her to London to be part of her family. Erica was a psychologist, her husband was a colonel in the British army and a medical doctor. They had a daughter named Eva. From that time on, I've kept in touch with this wonderful family."

Was the threat of death worth the preservation of this photo of your mother? I asked. Zahava answers unequivocally, "I simply couldn't bear to be totally cut off from my family. I needed some small tie to them. I kept the photo of my mother's face either stuck to my foot, in my shoe, or in my mouth, for the entire time." It was with her still when the camp was liberated at last—and is to this day.

AFTERWORD:
REMEMBRANCE

All four of my grandparents were European-born Jews. Three were originally Russian. My maternal grandmother claimed she was born in the same place in which Pushkin had been born. My maternal grandfather was born in Prelucki, near Kiev. My paternal grandfather was from Brody in Galicia, and my paternal grandmother was born in what was then also part of Austria-Hungary but is now part of the Czech Republic, Brno. All came to the United States in the early part of the twentieth century when they were quite young (some with, some without, parents), leaving a multitude of parents, grandparents, uncles, aunts, cousins in the Old World with whom contact was kept by letter until World War II broke out.

The last letter received by my paternal grandfather, written in Yiddish by his sister, loosely translated, follows in part:

August 17, 1939, Kostopol

To my dear, loved, highly respected brother Zalmen and my dear, loved, highly respected sister-in-law and your dear, loved, sweet children.

First, I wish to send all of you wishes for the new year which will soon be coming. All of you should be healthy, rich, and happy and we should hear one from the other. . . . I can write that your 70 zlotys I received before Pesach, for which I am very grateful to you. . . . I ask you very much, my dear brother, don't forget me and help me because I spent twenty dollars because I had to travel to see my sick child. Who else will take an interest in him but I who suffers so this poor life, always myself burdened with various troubles. Therefore I ask you to pity me and not forget me and therefore the living God will help you in the New Year. He will return to you a thousand times as much. And God should help us also be happy and we should also write joyful letters so my brother will have peace and my child, with God's help, will come home healthy. . . . I and my children greet you and kiss you with a very warm heart and wish you a good happy year.

From me, your sister . . .

Less than two weeks later World War II began. Not another word was ever heard from my grandfather's sister or anyone else in the Old World after the war. It was as if their very existence had been erased, which—as the world would eventually learn in more and more detail—was more or less what had been done to Jewish people like them and most likely to them. As a child growing up, there was nothing unusual in having grandparents who spoke English with an accent. (My peers in postwar New York were mainly descendants of Irish, Italian, Jewish immigrants, with grandparents or parents speaking, as my grandparents did, with colorful, sometimes comic—to us children—accents.) In my memory, almost nothing was ever mentioned in our family about these blood relations who'd been obliterated/erased in Europe.

(About as little was said about the Holocaust.) There were never discussions, and later—when I asked—I learned that although attempts were made to reconnect to surviving members of our family, no information was ever received. Of course the geography of Eastern Europe had also been altered, borders redrawn.

Then, one day in the 1970s, my aunt Dorothy's doorbell rang and a man with a heavy European accent identified himself as her cousin Zvi, originally from Russia. Being a savvy New Yorker, my aunt cracked her door ever so slightly to have a peek. Cynically, for good reason, she replied that this was not very likely, since she had no cousins alive in the Old World. The man she saw was a stocky, short powerhouse of a man and—cynicism aside—his physical appearance bowled her over because he was the spitting image of her father. So Dorothy let this "stranger" into her apartment. He explained that his father and her father had been half-brothers—the same father but different mothers. He related to Dorothy that after Sam/Zalmen, my grandfather, his uncle, had gone to America, his extended family remained in the small Russian city of Brody. However, when the odor of war with Germany steeped their city, his father had sent him, Zvi, east into Russia, away from impending danger, accompanied by a distant relative.

He'd been in his teens at the time, but in 1941, when Hitler broke the German–Russian nonaggression pact and war between the two countries had actually been declared, he'd lied about his age and volunteered to fight with the Red Army against Germany. He'd fought for the rest of the war, was in fact covered in scars. At war's end, he'd gone home and discovered that no one he knew was alive in his small city, so he'd joined a group of young people. (Yes, he was still a teenager.) Eventually, he made it to

Israel on one of the first illegal Exodus ships. He'd lived in Israel since, had fought in six wars, had a wife, three children. His family was growing and expanding.

Although my family had long assumed that we had no living relations across the sea, that the Ukrainian relatives had most likely been part of the murder of 33,000 Jews at the ravine of Babi Yar in September 1941, and the various other branches had met their ends in equally grim manners in slaughters, camps or gassings, shot and dumped into the River Dnieper, the Bug River, almost forty years after the end of World War II, we welcomed this tough, colorful Hebrew-speaking Israeli with an uncanny resemblance to our Russian grandfather, as well as his family, into our small, now totally Americanized tribe. Despite obliterating our extended family, Hitler had failed to erase us completely, because—against so many odds—one link in our family had managed to survive and, by going to the trouble of coming to New York and making an exhaustive search to find Aunt Dorothy, Cousin Zvi had reconnected himself to our slim chain and we to his.

Somehow years after this reunion it became my job and my passion to chronicle and salvage endangered/perishable stories from this time and place before they were erased by time. In gathering them, preserving their memory, I've become a catalyst/channel, an annotator of anguish. The cruelty and bitterness of this war will outlive us all although the number of survivors diminishes daily. Since I began this book, Rena has succumbed to Alzheimer's and has been placed in a nursing home. Luckily, just in time, she'd collaborated with a writer named Heather Dune Macadam on a memoir called *Rena's Promise*. Although she still speaks about her mother, she no longer knows her own name. Her sister Danka has Alzheimer's as well.

On May 27, 2002, I received the following e-mail from Israel:

Dear Alison,

With much sorrow we have to tell you that our father is no longer with us. After 4 very hard months of fighting, his kidneys betrayed him. They couldn't stand the stress. It is a very big loss and it is very hard to comprehend his going. Our parents were so special that now what we have left is a big hole. The funeral was yesterday and hundreds of people came to say goodbye to him. He loved people and he was loved by everyone who knew him.

Hadasa and Clila, children of Joseph Bau

In December I received this e-mail from Holland:

Dear Alison,

The first night I was with my daughter and a group of a hundred people in Warsaw to visit the extermination camps I fell sick by a heart attack with an infection at the lungs. I was in the hospital for more than two weeks. Now I am at home again but I feel weakly. You can say that I survived twice Poland! When I am able to do more than now I let you know.

Warm greetings from Jules (Schelvis)

I n eulogy to the victims of this war—dead and alive—are sewn the last patches into this quilted journey. Afterward, I will leave this war—all war, all cruelty, all bitterness, all anguish, all death—to turn my gaze toward blushing apricots that are ripening in a strong, healthy, leaf-festooned tree before my eyes on this late spring morning. Each of my subjects has made some indelible impression on me, either in person or through their writings. To end this bitter journey—like a trail of breadcrumbs—I leave you with the words of these survivors at the place where their road is ending.

Excerpt from Leo Bretholz's letter to Sister Jeanne d'Arc, Centre Hospitalier Régional de Limoges, 1998:

In your profession as a nurse you have met and cared for thousands of people, I'm sure. You would be hard-pressed to recall every case. But I shall never forget the moment when I first found myself in your presence. On May 8, 1944, an ambulance delivered me to the hospital with a strangulated hernia. My nom de guerre *was then Henri Lefèvre. I was a Jew, working with the Resistance, hoping to survive under an assumed identity. I feared that during surgery my Jewishness would be discovered. When I awoke, a gentle, whispering voice, close to my ear, was speaking to me in these comforting and reassuring words: "As long as I am in this ward, you have nothing to fear."*

I knew then that I had met an angel. It was you who had whispered these words of succor and compassion. I shall never forget them. Nor shall I forget your cheerful demeanor when you tended your patients' needs, sometimes whistling lifting tunes. Do you still whistle now? I hope this letter finds you in good health and fine spirits.

Excerpt from letter from Sister Jeanne d'Arc, Castres, France, to Leo Bretholz, Baltimore, November 1998:

You will never know how much your letter has touched me. And to think of the trouble you took to find my address. I was not able to respond im-

mediately—and will you please excuse me—because I have changed my situation. I have gone from being a nurse to becoming a patient myself, which is not at all conducive to engaging in correspondence.

But, do believe me, I have not lost the feeling of friendship which binds me to the sick. I am happy to have been of help to you, to give you comfort and take you into my prayers, at a time when there was so much hatred around you.

I no longer can hear very well. I can't even hear the ringing of the telephone next to my bed. But it will amuse you to know that I can still whistle, and I am going to try it, right now.

On this pleasant note, thank you again for your memories. Think of me as one who no longer resembles the sister-nurse of many years ago, but as the infirm sister who sends you her affection, for the pleasure you have given her by remembering.

Adina Blady Szwajger:

When I finished the last page of my memoirs, I went back to the beginning. I read them through—suddenly realized that something was wrong.

I had wanted to bear witness to the true events of those times, but I had done it very awkwardly.

Over the last forty-five years, the world has changed, new generations have grown up, and everything that happened has faded in the mists of history or even prehistory.

Everything has changed—even the streets I wrote about are no longer on the map of contemporary Warsaw. So much of what I wrote has ceased to be clear and comprehensible. Only for one man here in Poland (Marek Edelman) and a few dozen—maybe a score—around the world, my words are clear, and tell something we know about.

But those are not the important ones. We have crossed the barrier of shadows, and one by one we are leaving. The young are left behind. And it would be a good thing if something of those years remained for them. And so we need to explain, not just to reminisce. I don't know whether I am able to. I am not a professional writer, or a chronicler. But I must try—try to add a bit of history to what I remember.

Words of Eric Newby:

That night something happened to me on the mountain. The weight of the rice coupled with the awful cough which I had to try and repress broke something in me. It was not physical; it was simply that part of my spirit went out of me, and in the whole of my life since that night it has never been the same again.

ACKNOWLEDGMENTS

Because of my experience as a writer of Holocaust-related books over the past fifteen years I've gained exceptional access and have been trusted and entrusted by many survivors of this time. I am grateful for this trust and am passing it along to you. Although more than half a century has passed since many of these experiences were lived, the telling has not become easier. In some cases, the reflection of old age is felt through an even thinner skin, and the pain and loss remains razor-sharp. My gratitude deepens. For some of the subjects in this book, it's already too late. Believing that their stories belong here, I've made do with writings they've left behind, memoirs, interviews and other related materials.

Because of the crushing finality of time, it's unlikely that many young children will ever meet a living survivor of this time. Great urgency has been added to the gathering of these wrenching materials as their numbers are dwindling, their epoch is fading, their circle is closing. Each and every survivor in one way or other believes that his or her survival (what Martin Gilbert calls the "tainted luck" of survival) was astonishing. But they also bear a sense of guilt over why they and not another survived. Their—and my—bereavement for those who didn't survive is without end.

ACKNOWLEDGMENTS

Although the lion's share of this book deals with the Holocaust and Jewish threnody, innocent people of all stripes also suffered during and after the years 1939 through 1945 known as World War II. As the time of summing up is here, none should be excluded from the memorializing. The tragedy of all suffering and the marvel of any survival—in my mind—remain entwined. Thus I've mixed non-Jewish subjects in with Jewish subjects. I've even included one subject who was the son of a Nazi, guiltless of his father's complicity. I believe that his interrupted youth, his victimization, like so many other innocent civilians, should be remembered too. It must be underscored, as well, that people who survived were no more righteous or deserving or loved by (a theoretical or even a literal) God than those who didn't; that the mystery of fate's/God's/the Universe's choice is and remains evermore just that.

On a personal note, I thank my friends Danielle A. Durkin, Aine O'Healy, Eric Saul, Mark F. Walter, my editor Sara Carder, and my friend and agent Leslie Daniels for the precious metal of their time and their kind help.

I dedicate this book to another bountiful source of wealth—my sisters, Nancy and Maggie.

BIBLIOGRAPHY AND PERMISSIONS

I am indebted to and acknowledge the following books and their authors, translators and publishers whose work is used as source material, and for those who gave their kind permission to quote excerpts.

Bau, Joseph, *Dear God, Have You Ever Gone Hungry?*, trans. Shlomo "Sam" Youman (New York: Arcade, 1998). Excerpts reprinted by permission of Arcade Publishing.

Bretholz, Leo, with Michael Olesker, *Leap into Darkness* (New York: Random House/Anchor Books, 1999). Excerpts reprinted by permission of the authors.

Bruchfeld, Stéphane, and Paul A. Levine, *Tell Ye Your Children* . . . (Stockholm: Regeringskansliet, 2002).

Debenedetti, Giacomo, and Estelle Gilson, *October 16, 1943* and *Eight Jews*, trans. Estelle Gilson (Notre Dame, Ind.: University of Notre Dame Press, 2001).

Fralon, José-Alain, *A Good Man in Evil Times*, trans. Peter Graham (New York: Carroll & Graf, 1998).

Ganor, Solly, *Light One Candle* (New York: Kodansha International Press, 1995). Excerpts reprinted by permission of the author.

Gary, Romain, *Promise at Dawn* (New York: Pocket Books, 1961). Excerpts reprinted by permission of the Estate of Romain Gary.

Gelissen, Rena Kornreich, with Heather Dune Macadam, *Rena's Promise* (Boston: Beacon Press, 1995). Excerpts reprinted by permission of Beacon Press.

Gilbert, Martin, *Holocaust Journey* (London: Phoenix Books, 1997).

Gilbert, Martin, *The Second World War: A Complete History* (New York: Henry Holt & Co., 1989).

Goyen, William, *The House of Breath* (Evanston, Ill.: Northwestern University Press, 1999). Excerpt reprinted by permission of Northwestern University Press.

Hilberg, Raul, *The Destruction of the European Jews* (New York: Harper & Row, 1961).

Jacobsen, Ruth, *Rescued Images* (New York: Mikaya Press, 2001). Excerpt reprinted by permission of the author.

Kagan, Juram, *Poland's Jewish Landmarks* (New York: Hippocrene Books, 2001).

Kambanellis, Iakovos, *Mauthausen: A Memoir*, trans. Gail Holst-Warhaft (Athens: Kedros Publishers, 1995). Excerpts reprinted by permission of the author.

Keneally, Thomas, *Schindler's List* (New York: Simon & Schuster, 1982).

Kohn, Nahum, and Howard Roiter, *A Voice from the Forest* (New York: Holocaust Publications, 1980). Excerpts reprinted by permission of the author.

Levi, Primo, *Survival in Auschwitz*, trans. Giulio Einaudi (New York: Collier Books, 1959).

Levin, Nora, *The Holocaust* (New York: Schocken Books, 1973).

Levy, Alan, *The Wiesenthal File* (London: Constable & Robinson, 1993). Excerpts reprinted by permission of Constable & Robinson Publishing, Ltd.

Milosz, Czeslaw, "And Yet the Books," trans. Robert Haas. Copyright 1988 by Czeslaw Milosz Royalties, Inc. Reprinted by permission of HarperCollins, Inc.

Newby, Eric, *Love and War in the Apennines* (London: Penguin Books, 1971). Excerpts reprinted by permission of HarperCollins, Inc.

Nye, Naomi Shihab, "Kindness," from *Words Under the Words: Selected Poems by Naomi Shihab Nye* (Portland, Oreg.: Far Corner Books, 1995). Copyright 1995. Reprinted by permission of Far Corner Books.

Pick, Hella, *Simon Wiesenthal: A Life in Search of Justice* (Boston: Northeastern University Press, 1996). Excerpts reprinted by permission of Northeastern University Press.

Richler, Mordecai, ed., *Writers on World War II* (New York: Alfred A. Knopf, 1991).

Richmond, Theo, *Konin: A Quest* (New York: Pantheon, 1995). Excerpts reprinted by permission of Random House, Inc.

Schelvis, Jules, *Binnen de Poorten*, trans. Senta Kushkulei-Engelstein and Gerda Baardman (The Netherlands: De Haan, 1982). Excerpts reprinted by permission of the author.

Shirer, William L., *The Rise and Fall of the Third Reich* (New York: Simon & Schuster, 1959).

Szpilman, Wladyslaw, *The Pianist*, trans. Anthea Bell (New York: St. Martin's Press, 1999). Copyright 1999. Excerpts reprinted by permission of St. Martin's Press, LLS.

Szwajger, Adina Blady, *I Remember Nothing More: The Warsaw Children's Hospital and the Jewish Resistance*, trans. Tasja Darowska and Danusia Stok (New York: Random House, 1980). Excerpts reprinted by permission of Random House, Inc.

Tschuy, Theo, *Dangerous Diplomacy* (Grand Rapids, Mich.: William B. Eerdmans, 2000).

Vrba, Rudolf, with Alan Bestic, *Escape from Auschwitz* (New Jersey: Barricade Books, 2002). Excerpts reprinted by permission of Barricade Books.

Vrba, Rudolf, with Alan Bestic, *I Cannot Forgive* (Vancouver, Can.: Regent College Publishing, 1964). Excerpts reprinted by permission of Regent College Publishing.

Vrkljan, Irena, *The Silk, the Shear and Marina; Or, About Biography*, trans. Sibelan Forrester and Celia Hawkesworth (Evanston, Ill.: Northwestern University Press, 1999). Excerpt reprinted by permission of the author.

Vrkljan-Krizic, Nada, *Karl Sirovy: Life and Work, 1896–1948* (Zagreb, Croatia: The Museum of Contemporary Art, 1996). Excerpt reprinted by permission of the author.

Yahil, Leni, *The Holocaust: The Fate of European Jewry*, trans. Ina Friedman and Haya Galai (New York: Oxford Universtiy Press, 1987).

Also, special thanks to Norma Fain Pratt, for translation from the Yiddish, and to Alan Cottrell, Richard N. Strange and Michael Tatham for permission to quote from Letters to the Editor to *The Times* of London.

All efforts have been made to secure permissions for all materials in this book.

ILLUSTRATION CREDITS